New Directions for
Institutional Research

J. Fredericks Volkwein
EDITOR-IN-CHIEF

Robert K. Toutkoushian
ASSOCIATE EDITOR

Overcoming Survey Research Problems

Stephen R. Porter
EDITOR

Number 121 • Spring 2004
Jossey-Bass
San Francisco

OVERCOMING SURVEY RESEARCH PROBLEMS
Stephen R. Porter (ed.)
New Directions for Institutional Research, no. 121
J. Fredericks Volkwein, Editor-in-Chief

NEW DIRECTIONS FOR INSTITUTIONAL RESEARCH (ISSN 0271-0579, electronic ISSN 1536-075X) is part of The Jossey-Bass Higher and Adult Education Series and is published quarterly by Wiley Subscription Services, Inc., A Wiley Company, at Jossey-Bass, 989 Market Street, San Francisco, California 94103-1741 (publication number USPS 098-830). Periodicals Postage Paid at San Francisco, California, and at additional mailing offices. POSTMASTER: Send address changes to New Directions for Institutional Research, Jossey-Bass, 989 Market Street, San Francisco, California 94103-1741.

SUBSCRIPTIONS cost $80.00 for individuals and $150.00 for institutions, agencies, and libraries. See order form at end of book.

EDITORIAL CORRESPONDENCE should be sent to J. Fredericks Volkwein, Center for the Study of Higher Education, Penn State University, 400 Rackley Building, University Park, PA 16801-5252.

New Directions for Institutional Research is indexed in *College Student Personnel Abstracts, Contents Pages in Education,* and *Current Index to Journals in Education* (ERIC).

Microfilm copies of issues and chapters are available in 16mm and 35mm, as well as microfiche in 105mm, through University Microfilms Inc., 300 North Zeeb Road, Ann Arbor, Michigan 48106-1346.

www.josseybass.com

Contents

EDITOR'S NOTES   1
Stephen R. Porter

1. Raising Response Rates: What Works?   5
Stephen R. Porter
This chapter discusses the theoretical literature on why people choose
to respond to a survey and then reviews the latest empirical research
on how survey administration and characteristics of a survey affect
response rates.

2. Web Surveys: Best Practices   23
Paul D. Umbach
Research professionals are beginning to recognize the benefits of conducting their surveys over the Web, but they often have not considered
the best method for soliciting responses. This chapter summarizes the
most recent literature on the best practices of Web survey implementation and offers practical advice for researchers.

3. Conducting Surveys on Sensitive Topics   39
John H. Pryor
Many institutions are surveying students about sensitive topics such as
alcohol and drug use, sexual behavior, and academic dishonesty. Yet
these can be some of the most difficult surveys to administer successfully, given reluctance on the part of respondents both to participate
and to provide truthful answers. An experienced practitioner of surveys
on these topics describes the literature in this area and his own experience in conducting these surveys.

4. Understanding the Effect of Prizes on Response Rates   51
Stephen R. Porter, Michael E. Whitcomb
Offering a prize for survey participation is a common method to raise
response rates in student surveys. This chapter describes the results of
a study that the authors conducted to test the impact of prizes on
response rates in a survey of high school students.

5. Multiple Surveys of Students and Survey Fatigue   63
Stephen R. Porter, Michael E. Whitcomb, William H. Weitzer
As the use of student surveys grows in assessment and institutional
research, institutional researchers must deal with the impact of multiple surveys on response rates. This chapter reviews the literature on
survey fatigue and summarizes a research project that indicates that
administering multiple surveys in one academic year can significantly
suppress response rates in later surveys.

6. Conducting Longitudinal Studies   75

Karen W. Bauer

Longitudinal studies have become more common in higher education because of an increased emphasis on assessment. Multiple contacts with students require different survey administration techniques than those used for simple one-shot surveys. Experienced practitioners of longitudinal surveys will relate the literature and their own experience in conducting successful longitudinal surveys.

7. Pros and Cons of Paper and Electronic Surveys   91

Stephen R. Porter

As new survey technologies emerge, researchers can be quick to adopt them without understanding the consequences. This chapter describes the different types of paper and electronic surveys currently available and their costs and benefits in terms of equipment and printing costs, demands on staff time, and ease of use.

INDEX   99

EDITOR'S NOTES

As assessment and planning have begun to play a larger role in higher education, survey research has become a major function of institutional research offices. Senior administrative staff and members of boards of trustees often demand survey data to inform their decision making, and survey data are often presented to students, faculty, and alumni to justify policy changes.

At the same time, many institutional research offices are facing dual pressures: falling response rates and the demand for surveys on almost every conceivable subject. As response rates among the general public have fallen nationally over the past several decades, student survey response rates have also fallen. Researchers face skepticism from policymakers and other constituencies when they present analyses based on surveys with low response rates. Increasingly, researchers in higher education need additional methods in order to increase, if not simply maintain, their survey response rates. Yet these methods may increase costs or may not be effective if used incorrectly.

The central role that survey research has come to play in the assessment and planning process has also fueled the demand for surveys on a wide variety of topics as well as for surveys with complex designs. Many institutional researchers must now implement surveys on behaviors that might be illegal or that violate school policies, such as alcohol use or cheating. Longitudinal surveys are also becoming more popular in higher education.

This volume of *New Directions for Institutional Research* examines several aspects of the survey research enterprise in higher education, with the aim of providing readers with ways in which to increase response rates while controlling costs. Many institutional researchers face additional demands in terms of survey research, from administering multiple surveys over time to administering surveys on sensitive subjects, such as student alcohol and drug use. New technologies for survey administration also provide many different options from which to choose. This volume discusses these issues in terms of the survey research literature as well as the experiences of practitioners in the field. Many institutional researchers may be unfamiliar with the vast survey research methodology literature, but this literature offers many helpful suggestions for designing survey instruments and survey administration. Although knowing the literature is helpful, advice from those in the field is invaluable, especially given the unique nature of one of our primary survey populations—college students.

Chapter One, by Stephen R. Porter, focuses on effective ways to improve response rates in surveys. It reviews the theoretical literature on why people choose to respond to a survey, as well as the latest empirical research on the impact of various aspects of surveys on response rates. Some of the topics covered are repeated contacts with respondents, survey length, personalization, promises of confidentiality and anonymity, and survey fatigue (of particular interest to institutional researchers given the multiple surveys we often conduct).

For those researchers who choose to go the electronic route, Chapter Two, by Paul D. Umbach, reviews the most recent literature on Web survey techniques. While Web surveys can offer significant cost savings over paper surveys, the method of implementation can be quite different from implementing paper surveys. This chapter summarizes the most recent literature on the best practices of Web survey implementation and offers practical advice for researchers.

Chapter Three, by John Pryor, examines the design and administration of sensitive surveys in higher education. Surveys that ask questions about sensitive behavior—such as alcohol and drug use, sexual behavior, or academic dishonesty—pose additional challenges compared to the typical student survey. An experienced practitioner discusses these challenges and his own experience in conducting these types of surveys.

Chapter Four, by Stephen R. Porter and Michael E. Whitcomb, considers the efficacy of awarding prizes for survey participation, one common method for raising response rates in student surveys. The survey research literature indicates that these prizes should have little effect. The authors use a survey of high school prospects to test the impact of prizes on response rates.

As the demand for surveys has increased, institutional research offices have responded by conducting more and more surveys. Chapter Five, by Stephen R. Porter, Michael E. Whitcomb, and William Weitzer, examines survey fatigue, one of the more pressing issues in the administration of student surveys. Using several student surveys conducted over two academic years, the authors estimate the impact of multiple survey administrations on response rates in later surveys.

Longitudinal surveys, such as the Higher Education Research Institute's Cooperative Institutional Research Program surveys and Your First College Year survey, and Indiana University's College Student Experiences Questionnaire and College Student Expectations Questionnaire, have recently become more common because of increased emphasis on assessment. Chapter Six, by Karen Bauer, reviews some of the research design and implementation issues for these types of surveys. An experienced practitioner of longitudinal surveys describes some of the literature and her own experience in conducting successful longitudinal surveys.

Chapter Seven discusses the various paper and electronic survey options now available to institutional researchers. Many offices face the decision of whether to move their student and faculty surveys to the Web. This chapter describes the different types of survey options currently available and their costs and benefits in terms of equipment and printing, demands on staff time, ease of use, response rates, and bias.

Together these chapters should be helpful to any researcher conducting surveys in higher education. The environment in which we conduct surveys is constantly changing and we must change our survey administration methods to adapt to this new environment. College students, for example, are now barraged with surveys from market researchers and at the same time are more Web-focused than were students a decade ago. Adapting our survey tools to an increasingly "noisy" survey environment and changing student and faculty populations will be a central challenge for institutional researchers in the coming years.

Stephen R. Porter
Editor

STEPHEN R. PORTER *is director of institutional research at Wesleyan University in Middletown, Conn.*

This chapter discusses the theoretical literature on why people choose to respond to a survey and reviews the latest empirical research on how survey administration and the characteristics of a survey affect response rates.

Raising Response Rates: What Works?

Stephen R. Porter

Surveys are one of the most important tools in the institutional research toolbox, and not surprisingly, survey research is one of the most common activities in institutional research (Schlitz, 1988). Surveys are now used in almost all facets of higher education planning, such as recruitment and admission of students, to describe the characteristics of an incoming class, assess student satisfaction and the collegiate experience, understand retention and graduation outcomes, and analyze alumni satisfaction and donor behavior. Demands for external assessment have also grown, fueling an increase in the demand for quality survey data to assess educational outcomes. Legislatures in some states (such as Maryland) are also using results from alumni surveys as the basis for performance indicators for state universities, tying funding to the amount of alumni satisfaction. More than ever, higher education professionals need quality survey data for internal and external assessment and planning.

At the same time as the demand for survey research has increased, however, survey response rates have been falling, both in the United States and in Europe (Atrostic, Bates, Burt, and Silberstein, 2001; Baruch, 1999; de Heer, 1999; Steeh, 1981). More disturbing is the common finding that these rates have been falling not only because it has become more difficult to contact people, but also because refusals to participate are also increasing. Although most of the research on falling response rates focuses on surveys of the general population, Dey (1997) shows that response rates in a set of national student surveys fell from around 60 percent in the 1960s to just 21 percent in the late 1980s. These declines may be due to many different factors, such as changing cultural norms for cooperation and an increase in academic and marketing surveys. One thing is clear: survey nonresponse has become a serious problem for researchers in higher education.

Why worry about low survey response rates? Unfortunately, survey nonresponse is usually not random and in turn may bias survey results (Groves, 1989). Those who choose not to respond to surveys of the general population, for example, tend to be less educated and older. My own experience with student surveys indicates that females, whites, and first- and second-year students are more likely to respond to surveys than are other student groups. To the extent that respondents differ from nonrespondents in attitudes and beliefs, surveys with low response rates will be unrepresentative of the population under study. Any conclusions drawn from such unrepresentative data may be erroneous, which is problematic when such data are used for planning purposes. While we can often measure the impact of nonresponse on demographic characteristics, its impact on survey results is usually unknown.

To correct for a low response rate, researchers have two choices. The first is to use a variety of measures to increase the response rate, such as multiple survey mailings, monetary incentives, or person-to-person follow-up of nonrespondents. Such measures can be expensive and drive up the costs of surveying. Second, the survey data can be weighted for nonresponse (Dey, 1997; Kalton, 1983), a process that adds an additional layer of complexity to any research project. Recommendations and analyses based on such weighted survey data may still be rejected, on the rationale that the response rates are so low that weighting cannot correct for the bias in the data.

The end result is that institutional researchers have developed a variety of measures to combat nonresponse, some of which may be effective, and some which may not. Many researchers may be unaware of the rich experimental literature on survey research techniques in other academic fields. This chapter reviews the current experimental literature on survey nonresponse to provide researchers in higher education with effective techniques for increasing response rates. Note the focus on experimental: all too often we focus on changes in response rates in a particular survey from year to year, yet such changes can occur for reasons other than a change in survey administration. By focusing on experimental testing we can be more confident that the new techniques we adopt will have a positive impact on response rates. With the demand for surveys increasing, survey response rates decreasing, and students questioning the relevance of our surveys (Asiu, Antons, and Fultz, 1998), it is more important than ever that researchers in higher education use the best tools available when collecting survey data.

Theories of Survey Response

Understanding why people respond to a survey is vital to both collectors and analysts of survey data. For researchers conducting a survey, a solid understanding of how respondents will perceive and react to a survey is essential to adapting survey research techniques to the particulars of the survey and institution. For researchers analyzing survey data, surveys cannot be appropriately adjusted for nonresponse without a theoretical framework to guide the weighting procedure (Couper and Groves, 1995).

Much of the literature on survey response has been atheoretical, with researchers conducting experiments based on practical experience to understand the effectiveness of a particular technique (Groves, Cialdini, and Couper, 1992). More recently, scholars have worked to develop an explicit theoretical framework for survey nonresponse. These theoretical approaches to survey participation can be divided into two general groups. The first group emphasizes some sort of reasoned action on the part of the potential participant, with calculations of the costs and benefits to survey participation. The second group emphasizes a psychological approach by viewing the decision to participate as a heuristic one; that is, the potential participant uses a set of simple rules to determine survey participation instead of devoting large amounts of thought to the decision to respond.

The reasoned action approach often relies on social exchange theory to explain why someone fills out a survey. As Dillman (2000, p. 14) states,

> Three elements are critical for predicting a particular action: rewards, costs, and trust. Simply stated, rewards are what one expects to gain from a particular activity, costs are what one gives up or spends to obtain the rewards, and trust is the expectation that in the long run the rewards of doing something will outweigh the costs. The theory of social exchange implies three questions about the design of a questionnaire and the implementation process: How can we increase rewards for responding? How can perceived costs be reduced? How can trust be established so that the ultimate rewards will outweigh the costs of responding?

Literature in this area (such as Dillman, 2000; Hox, de Leeuw, and Vorst, 1995) has tended to focus on different methods of survey administration and survey design to increase the probability of response. By offering monetary incentives with a survey, for example, or reducing survey length, the researcher can increase the benefits and reduce the costs of survey participation in the hopes of increasing the probability of response. Much of the work by Dillman (2000) has taken this approach to understanding and affecting survey response.

The psychological approach has emphasized the informal decision rules or "rules of thumb" that respondents use when deciding to participate. For example, "the survey request situation most often favors a heuristic approach because the potential respondent typically does not have a large personal interest in survey participation and, consequently, is not inclined to devote large amounts of time or cognitive energy to the decision of whether to participate" (Groves, Cialdini, and Couper, 1992, p. 480). Groves, Cialdini, and Couper (1992) identify several heuristic factors that may play a role in survey nonresponse, including the norm of reciprocity, helping tendencies, compliance with legitimate authority, and perceptions of scarcity.

People may be more likely to respond if a norm of reciprocity has been established between themselves and the person or entity administering the survey. Such a norm directs that people should treat others as they have been treated, so if someone has provided a benefit or favor, some sort of reciprocal benefit should in turn be provided. This understanding of human interaction helps explain why the inclusion of a one dollar bill with a survey usually increases survey response, because a dollar is too small a sum to be viewed as raw compensation for filling out the survey.

In addition, Groves, Cialdini, and Couper (1992) posit that simple helping tendencies, or a norm of social responsibility, also affect the survey response decision. People may respond positively to a request not because of reciprocal behavior but because the person has simply requested their assistance. This leads to the idea that requests for help by filling out the survey should feature predominantly in survey cover letters.

Two other psychological concepts are also useful in understanding survey response. First, people are more likely to comply with a request when it comes from an authority viewed as legitimate. This tendency leads many academic and governmental organizations to emphasize their sponsorship of a survey. Second, scarce opportunities are often perceived as more valuable than common opportunities, so emphasizing to respondents that they are part of a select group should increase response rates.

From this discussion we can see that the two modes—reasoned action and psychological—are distinct in how they approach cognitive behavior, but they also overlap and often use similar concepts when applying theory to understanding survey nonresponse. Groves, Cialdini, and Couper (1992), for example, use the concept of scarcity and value in their discussion of compliance behaviors, while Dillman (2000) emphasizes informing respondents that opportunities to respond are scarce in order to encourage response. Nonetheless, these two distinct views of the survey response are important to keep in mind when devising strategies to combat nonresponse. People certainly take into account costs when deciding to fill out a survey; if they did not, we would all be sending out one-hundred-page survey questionnaires. Yet not all reactions to a request to participate in a survey are calculated: some are psychological and rely on simple rules of thumb when making the decision to participate, such as responding only when the survey's cover letter contains a simple request for help. Both approaches must be borne in mind when designing and implementing a survey.

Techniques to Combat Nonresponse

This section summarizes research on factors that can affect response rates, such as mode, number of contacts, survey length, incentives, salience, confidentiality, survey sponsorship, and deadlines.

Paper Versus Web. Probably one of the most common questions an educational researcher faces today is whether to conduct a survey on the Internet. Web surveys can offer several advantages, such as shorter administration time, lower costs, and fewer data-entry errors. Yet some researchers question the validity of data obtained from Web surveys; a common finding, for example, is that responses from Web surveys tend to show more positive outcomes for computer- and technology-related items (Carini, Hayek, Kuh, Kennedy, and Ouimet, 2003). More important, many researchers worry that their response rate will fall if they switch from paper to Web surveys. Numerous studies have compared response rates on mail and Web surveys, and the results are mixed. This is a consequence of the difficulty in drawing conclusions about response rates from such studies. Web surveys may do poorly not because paper surveys simply have higher response rates; instead, many results may be due to the research design. For example, some scholars have compared response rates for the same survey across years, after the survey administration has changed from paper to Web (Roscoe, Terkla, and Dyer, 2002). Yet changes in response rates from year to year may be due to causes other than mode.

Another example is a widely cited study by Mehta and Sivadas (1995) that looks at response rates for paper (mail) and e-mail surveys. Although the authors find a higher response rate for their paper survey groups than for their e-mail groups, a close examination of their experiment reveals differences between their experimental groups other than survey mode. One paper group received a $1 incentive while the comparison e-mail group did not, probably causing much, if not all, of the 20 percentage point difference. In another of their paper versus e-mail experiments, a rash of complaints about unsolicited e-mails caused them to shut down the e-mail portion of the experiment early. Close attention must be paid to the structure of an experiment before drawing any conclusions about response rates.

Even experiments that appear similar can show contradictory results. Four different studies using samples of faculty found that a Web survey yielded response rates 18 percentage points higher (Cobanoglu, Warde, and Moreo, 2001), .5 percentage points higher (Schaefer and Dillman, 1998), 1 percentage point lower (Weible and Wallace, 1998), and 15 percentage points lower (Shannon and Bradshaw, 2002) than a paper survey.

These contradictory results are no doubt due to characteristics of the sample as well as to the survey design. As described in Chapter Two, a Web survey will be successful only if the population has easy access to the Internet and is comfortable with using the Web, and if the researcher has accurate e-mail addresses. Clearly there is a generational component to e-mail usage (Mitra, Hazen, LaFrance, and Rogan, 1999), the most common method of contact in Web surveys. E-mail and computer usage will also vary between institutions. One study found a lower response rate for the Web version of the survey, but focus group discussions revealed that some students ignored their university e-mail account in favor of other e-mail providers (such as Hotmail), and that students who did not have home computers had difficulty accessing computers on campus (Handwerk, Carson, and Blackwell, 2000). Design aspects of a Web survey can also affect response rates. Surveys with a "fancy" appearance have lower response rates than plain surveys (Dillman, Tortora, Conradt, and Bowker, 1998), and surveys that require the respondent to key an identification number and password into the survey have lower response rates than surveys that automatically log in the respondent (Crawford, Couper, and Lamias, 2001).

The end result is that Web survey response rates will depend very much on the institutional context as well as on the ability of the researcher to conduct a well-designed electronic survey. My own experience at two institutions has been very positive, and my office now uses Web surveys whenever possible. At the same time, we have also devoted significant resources to Web survey design, such as working with our information technology office to develop a way for respondents to be automatically logged into our surveys. Web surveys can yield large response rates, but only after careful consideration of the survey population and design of the survey instrument.

Multiple Contacts. One of the most successful techniques to increase response rates is the use of multiple contacts with members of the sample. This technique was developed and refined by Dillman (2000), and is now considered standard methodology for any survey.

Generally, researchers use one of two types of contacts in any survey administration: either a stand-alone message or the survey instrument accompanied by a message. Stand-alone messages include prenotification contacts (in which the respondent is contacted prior to receiving a survey and is informed about the upcoming survey administration) and reminder notices such as postcards. Examples of messages with surveys include a cover letter accompanied by a copy of the survey questionnaire (sent initially or a second or third time to nonrespondents) or an e-mail containing a hyperlink to a survey Web site. Prenotifications inform respondents that the survey will be arriving, reducing the chance that the survey or e-mail will be inadvertently thrown away. Postcard reminders and multiple copies of the survey instrument sent to nonrespondents remind them to complete the survey if their nonresponse is due simply to being too busy or forgetful. Multiple contacts may also increase the legitimacy of the survey (Fox, Crask, and Kim, 1988).

To derive full benefit from multiple contacts, researchers should use a prenotification message followed by a copy of the survey with a cover message (a reminder sent to all respondents shortly after they receive the copy of the survey), followed finally by one or more contacts with nonrespondents using combined messages and surveys (Dillman, 2000; Dillman and Bowker, 2001).

Obviously, multiple contacts will increase the costs and time involved with a survey, raising the question of effectiveness. Numerous studies indicate that stand-alone messages are well worth the effort. Experiments using samples of the general population found that prenotification letters increased response rates by 4 percentage points (Brehm, 1994), 6 percentage points (Dillman, Clark, and Sinclair, 1995), and 16 percentage points (Goldstein and Jennings, 2002). Results from meta-analyses estimate the impact of a prenotification letter on response rates to be about 8 percentage points (Fox, Crask, and Kim, 1988; Yu and Cooper, 1983), or to increase response rates by 29 percent (Yammarino, Skinner, and Childers, 1991). Reminder postcards have also been shown to increase response rates. Dillman, Clark, and Sinclair (1995) estimate an increase in response rates of 8 percentage points in their study, while a meta-analysis of previous studies demonstrated an effect size on response rates of 3.5 percent (Fox, Crask, and Kim, 1988).

Research also shows that increasing the number of surveys sent to respondents increases response rates. James and Bolstein (1990) found that mailing a fourth survey increased the response rate by more than 30 percentage points. From a higher education perspective, two survey mailings versus one survey mailing to alumni increased response rates 12 to 20 percentage points (Smith and Bers, 1987). Looking at the overall number of contacts (regardless of type), two meta-analyses confirm their impact. Heberlein and Baumgartner (1978) and Goyder (1982) find that each additional contact increases responses rates in the range of 7 to 11 percentage points.

Another example of the impact of multiple contacts on a survey administered in an academic setting is shown in Figure 1.1. A Web survey about university rental housing was administered to faculty and staff at Wesleyan University in the fall of 2002. After the first e-mail notification, the response rate was leveling off at around 44 percent (this high rate reflects the effect of the prenotification e-mail from the university provost as well as the high salience of the survey). After an e-mail reminder was sent to nonrespondents, the response rate increased to 67 percent, and a final reminder to nonrespondents notifying them of the deadline for the survey resulted in a final response rate of almost 72 percent, substantially higher than the rate after the first e-mail notification.

While they often increase costs, multiple contacts with respondents are one of the best ways to ensure a good response rate. This is one reason that Web surveys are growing in popularity: three or four contacts with respondents can be costless, while three or four paper mailings can be quite expensive, especially if postage is required.

Length. Excessive survey questionnaire length is also viewed by many researchers as an inhibitor to response (Bogen, 1996), because longer surveys take more time to fill out and thus increase the costs to the respondent. Respondents may fill out only part of the survey, or very long surveys may simply be rejected outright when first viewed.

In general, the experimental research on mail surveys indicates that shorter surveys do elicit higher response rates, but many of the differences

Figure 1.1. Electronic Mailings and Response Rates (Housing Survey)

	Th	Fr	Sa	Su	Mo	Tu	We	Th	Fr	Sa	Su	Mo
Cumulative %	0.0%	26.6%	27.9%	29.0%	39.4%	43.9%	61.7%	66.0%	67.0%	67.0%	67.0%	71.5%
Daily %	0.0%	26.6%	1.3%	1.1%	10.4%	4.5%	17.8%	4.3%	1.1%	0.0%	0.0%	4.5%

Day of the Week

are quite small. One study using U.S. Census Bureau forms of varying lengths found that the response rates for the short and medium forms were similar (70–71 percent), but higher than the response rate for the long form (67 percent) (Dillman, Sinclair, and Clark, 1993). The short and medium survey forms consisted of a half-page (one-side) and a single sheet (both sides), respectively, while the long form was an eight-page booklet. Increasing the number of pages from two to eight caused response rates to drop only about 3 to 4 percentage points. A study by Statistics Norway using a large mail survey found that response rates dropped from 63 percent for a two-page questionnaire to 54 percent for an eight-page questionnaire (Haraldsen, Stalnacke, and Fosen, 1999). Similar results hold for interview length (Groves, Singer, Corning, and Bowers, 1999; Sharp and Frankel, 1983).

Several meta-analyses of surveys also indicate that the impact of length is a modest negative effect. In their analysis of 98 studies, Heberlein and Baumgartner (1978) estimate a 5 percent reduction in response rates for every additional ten pages of questionnaire. Similarly, Yammarino, Skinner, and Childers (1991) examined 115 studies and found that response rates fell by about 8 percent for surveys greater than four pages in length. Yu and Cooper (1983) found a negative correlation between length and response rate in their meta-analysis of 93 articles, but the correlation was very weak ($r = -0.06$).

Thus, while survey length appears correlated with nonresponse, the effect is rather moderate. So how long is too long? Two surveys of undergraduate students' attitudes toward surveys yield similar answers. A survey of Air Force Academy cadets asked students the ideal length of a survey, with students on average stating twenty-two questions and thirteen minutes or less to complete (Asiu, Antons, and Fultz, 1998). Another survey of undergraduates at a public university yielded an average response of thirteen minutes to complete (Handwerk, Carson, and Blackwell, 2000). Both studies indicate that college students prefer relatively short surveys.

Incentives. Incentives are a common way to increase response rates. While substantial sums of money are occasionally offered as compensation for survey participation, small token sums are usually offered to invoke the norm of reciprocity. Yet contrary to popular belief, only certain types of incentives affect response rates. Prepaid incentives (enclosed with the survey itself) consistently raise response rates, while postpaid incentives (paid upon completion of the survey) do not.

Numerous experiments and meta-analyses demonstrate the impact of prepaid incentives, usually in the form of a $1 bill enclosed with the survey (Church, 1993; Fox, Crask, and Kim, 1988; Heberlein and Baumgartner, 1978; Warriner and others, 1996; Willimack, Schuman, Pennell, and Lepkowski, 1995; Yammarino, Skinner, and Childers, 1991). Nonmonetary incentives of low value (such as a ballpoint pen) also positively affect response rates (Willimack, Schuman, Pennell, and Lepkowski, 1995).

The impact of prepaid incentives is both statistically and substantively significant. For example, in their meta-analysis Heberlein and Baumgartner (1978) found that a $1 prepayment increased response rates by about 24 percent; Yammarino, Skinner, and Childers (1991) estimated that the inclusion of $.50 increased response rates by 18 percent, while incentives of $1 or more increased response rates by 12 percent. An experimental study using a thirty-page questionnaire found that inclusion of $2 increased response rates by 8.7 percentage points over the control (no incentive group), and $5 increased response rates by 13.8 percentage points over the control group (Warriner and others, 1996). Another experimental study found that a prepayment of $5 increased response rates by 23.7 percentage points (Groves, Singer, and Corning, 2000).

Similarly, numerous studies demonstrate that postpaid incentives have no impact on response rates (Berk, Mathiowetz, Ward, and White, 1987; Berry and Kanouse, 1987; Church, 1993; Cook, Heath, and Thompson, 2000; James and Bolstein, 1992; see also Chapter Four in this volume). The difference lies in how the payment is viewed by survey recipients.

Payment conditional on survey participation makes the incentive appear as compensation for the time and effort involved in filling out and returning the survey. This can affect survey response in two related ways. First, the incentive does not appear as a gift, so the survey recipient does not feel as if a favor or benefit has been granted by the survey sender; thus the norm of reciprocity is not invoked. Because the incentive is now viewed as pure compensation and because even postpaid incentives are invariably quite small in value, the amount of incentive is not sufficient to compensate for the time and effort involved (for most individuals). Note that in this scenario postpayments should increase response rates if they are sufficiently large, but the amounts necessary appear to be outside the budgets of most institutional researchers (for example, a $50 postpayment offered to members of a national trade association yielded a statistically insignificant increase of 3 percentage points; see James and Bolstein, 1992).

In addition, any consideration of incentives must balance the cost of such incentives against other techniques that improve response rates, such as multiple contacts. Researchers should also be aware of the impact of incentives on expectations in future surveys on campus, although research on the general population (Singer, van Hoewyk, and Maher, 1998, 2000) indicates that this is not an issue.

Survey Salience. Salience is simply how important or relevant a survey topic is to the survey recipient. Unfortunately, survey salience may be out of the researcher's hands and dictated by project needs; nevertheless, it is useful to understand the effects of salience when designing both surveys and cover messages.

In their meta-analysis, Heberlein and Baumgartner (1978) quantified the salience of the surveys in their study using a three-point scale (salient, possibly salient, or nonsalient). Surveys were coded as salient if the topic dealt with issues that were both important and current, such as a Veterans Affairs survey of educational interests of veterans, while surveys that did not deal with both important and current issues, such as a survey asking questions about socioeconomic status, were coded as nonsalient. Heberlein and Baumgartner found a 14.6 percent difference in response rates between salient and nonsalient surveys, while a follow-up study by Goyder (1982) found a difference of 12.2 percent.

A study by Groves, Singer, and Corning (2000) used an initial survey to develop measures of community involvement, and then mailed a follow-up survey about assisted suicide to the first-wave completers, hypothesizing higher response rates from those who scored high on their community involvement scale. They found a 14.9 percentage point difference between the low and high community involvement scales.

Salience is an important factor in respondent behavior; unfortunately, it is also one aspect of a survey that is difficult to alter. This research suggests that, at a minimum, salience should be emphasized in messages accompanying a survey.

Statements of Confidentiality. Researchers often believe that a statement of confidentiality should be included with a survey to encourage truthful responses and increase response rates (Dillman, Singer, Clark, and Treat, 1996; Singer, von Thurn, and Miller, 1995). Providing an assurance of confidentiality to the respondent may lower the perceived cost of their response being made public and should also foster a sense of trust, both key elements in the social exchange view of survey response behavior. Yet such statements could also decrease response rates by heightening respondents' awareness of what might happen to their survey responses. (Note that this discussion treats as voluntary the decision to include an assurance of confidentiality and ignores the possibility that such a statement may be required by an institutional review board.)

In their meta-analysis of thirty research studies, Singer, von Thurn, and Miller (1995) found mixed support overall for the hypothesis that confidentiality assurances affect survey response. Taking a more detailed look by classifying their studies on the basis of whether sensitive information was being asked, they discovered that such assurances do indeed have a positive impact on both unit and item response rates, but only when the survey asks for information about behaviors that are illegal or generally viewed with disapproval. Their calculated effect was small, however, indicating that such statements will have only a small impact on increasing response rates.

Furthermore, the distinction between sensitive and nonsensitive information is important. Strong statements of confidentiality can backfire when used with nonsensitive survey instruments, actually reducing response rates (Singer, Hippler, and Schwarz, 1992). Such strong statements lead potential respondents to believe that the survey will ask sensitive or embarrassing questions, which in turn leads them to decline to participate.

Requests for Help. If people tend to follow a norm of social responsibility, they may be more likely to comply with a survey request couched in terms of asking for help. Some evidence indicates that this is indeed the case. Mowen and Cialdini (1980) report an 18 percentage point increase by including the phrase "it would really help us out" in their communications. Conversely, we recently tried an experiment at Wesleyan University with a Web survey of prospective students who had visited campus, and found no statistically significant impact from using similar language. In part this result may be due to the proliferation of spam, which causes prospective students to discount e-mail communications.

This is clearly an area where more research is needed, especially in higher education. With many research projects in institutional research constrained by budgets and topic salience, the cover message is one factor that can be altered easily and without any cost.

Sponsorship. Research shows that, in general, surveys sponsored by governmental or academic organizations achieve higher response rates than surveys conducted by commercial businesses. Meta-analyses indicate that this difference is in the range of 9 to 14 percentage points (Fox, Crask, and Kim, 1988; Goyder, 1982; Heberlein and Baumgartner, 1978). This is of course good news for academic researchers. Yet, like salience, it is also an aspect of a survey that cannot be altered.

One issue that many institutional researchers face is determining who the survey sponsor is *within* an institution. Should the institutional research office list itself as the sponsor on a health survey, or should the health service office be listed? My literature review did not reveal any research on this question. A Web survey of high school students conducted by a colleague and myself found no difference in response rates between those students contacted via e-mail by the admissions office and those students contacted by the institutional research office (Porter and Whitcomb, 2002).

Institutional researchers who hire external organizations to administer a survey should take care to emphasize the connection to their institution, especially if the external organization is commercial. It is unclear whether sponsorship by different organizational units within a college or university has an impact on response rates.

Deadlines. The perception of scarcity can influence response rates, because people have a tendency to view scarce opportunities as more valuable than more common opportunities. In terms of survey research, giving respondents a deadline should also increase participation, because the time frame for participation is limited.

Results in this area are mixed, with experimental studies finding both positive and negative effects (such as Dossett, Latham, and Saari, 1980; Roberts, McCrory, and Forthofer, 1978). Several meta-analyses indicate that deadlines have no impact on response rates (Fox, Crask, and Kim, 1988; Yammarino, Skinner, and Childers, 1991; Yu and Cooper, 1983).

Conversely, an experiment using a Web survey of high school students found that inclusion of both a deadline and a statement of selectivity (for example, "You are one of a small group chosen. . . . ") increased response rates by 8 percentage points (Porter and Whitcomb, 2002). Thus it appears that inclusion of a deadline in a cover letter will not decrease the response rate but will most likely not increase it either.

Environment and Background. Finally, we should bear in mind the unique economic and social environments of our respective institutions. Some researchers may achieve particularly high or low response rates at an institution simply due to some particular characteristic of the student body or faculty. Interestingly, research on regional cooperation rates in the U.S. decennial census show that urban, densely populated, and high-crime areas all tend to have lower cooperation rates (Couper and Groves, 1996). Another study used estimates of socioeconomic status based on housing to demonstrate that the probability of survey participation is likelier for people with higher socioeconomic status (Goyder, Warriner, and Miller, 2002). This research suggests that despite our best efforts, it simply may not be possible to achieve a high survey response rate at some institutions.

Discussion

This review of the literature on survey response rates presents a picture of what we know about survey methodology and survey nonresponse. In sum,

- Survey administration via the Web may yield response rates on par with or even greater than paper administration, but it depends on the population under study and the design of the Web survey.

- Multiple contacts, both with and without inclusion of a survey, significantly increase response rates.
- Longer surveys yield lower response rates, but the effect is moderate.
- Incentives increase response rates only when they are included with the survey instrument; incentives conditional on survey completion have no effect on response rates.
- Highly salient surveys yield higher response rates.
- Statements of confidentiality affect response rates only when the survey contains sensitive questions; strong statements of confidentiality can actually decrease response rates for nonsensitive surveys.
- Requests for help in the cover letter may increase response rates.
- Surveys sponsored by academics yield higher response rates than surveys sponsored by commercial organizations.
- It is unclear whether the inclusion of a deadline affects response rates.
- The survey environment at a particular institution will affect the response rate.

This review suggests several ways in which researchers can structure a research project to achieve a high survey response rate. Often, however, it may not be possible to design and administer a survey that maximizes the probability of survey response in all of the areas listed here. When faced with constraints in some areas, researchers must use proven techniques in other areas to yield acceptable results.

For example, one of the more interesting—and for the institutional researcher, disheartening—results concerns salience. The impact of salience is disheartening because the subject of our surveys is usually driven by administrative needs and not by the desire to achieve a high response rate. But when faced with a low-salience survey, other aspects of the survey can be changed as a counterbalance. For example, the number of contacts can be increased, the length of the survey can be reduced by a page or two, and so on. In other words, researchers should leverage whichever aspects of the survey design and administration they can. And if for some reason this proves impossible, they will at least know beforehand and can inform others involved in the project that the response rate will quite likely be low.

The leveraging approach also suggests that surveys must be consciously designed and administered to increase response rates. This is not a truism. It is easy to develop a culture in which survey administration begins to change to meet the needs of the researcher rather than the needs of the respondent. Dillman (1996, for example, writes about the difficulty of innovation in government surveys and about how a culture can develop that does not use the results of the survey research literature to guide design decisions. He lists some common assumptions about survey design that are probably familiar to many institutional research offices (p. 118):

- Sending the questionnaires by bulk-rate postage will save money.
- It is more efficient not to put mailing dates on questionnaire cover letters and not to address them individually to people in the sample.
- Squeezing questions onto one page is OK even if the respondent is required to follow a rather serpentine path in order to read instructions and answer questions.
- It is desirable to use the same construction for all mail questionnaires regardless of content so that the same envelopes can be used.

Every survey must be designed to make the respondents' job of filling it out easier, not to make the job of administering surveys easier.

This approach also implies that we must constantly innovate in terms of how we collect survey data. As technologies change and student and faculty cultures change, we must be more than willing to change our methods. If we are not, the trends in response rates described at the beginning of the chapter will no doubt continue, to the detriment of our research enterprises.

Selected Survey Research Resources on the Web

The Web Survey Methodology Web site has an extensive bibliography of survey research papers, both academic and from the field of marketing: http://www.websm.org

The Survey Research Methods section of the American Statistical Association has a series of brochures about surveys and focus groups available online, as well as copies of their proceedings from 1978 to 2000: http://www.amstat.org/sections/srms

The American Association for Public Opinion Research has posted what they consider to be best practices for survey research as well as a set of standards for calculating response rates: http://www.aapor.org

NCS Pearson is an assessment and testing company that has available online an extensive series of research notes on surveying. If you ever want to know whether your scales should be even- or odd-numbered, you can find the answer here. The site also has a nice online sample-size and confidence-interval calculator: http://www.ncspearson.com/research-notes

Public Opinion Quarterly. This journal is published by the University of Chicago for the American Association of Public Opinion Research and features articles on public opinion and on theories and methods of survey research. Past issues are available through JSTOR (http://www.jstor.org) and you can sign up to be e-mailed the table of contents of new issues as they are published: http://www.journals.uchicago.edu/POQ/index.html

Journal of Official Statistics. This journal is published by Statistics Sweden, the national statistical office of Sweden, and features articles on methodologies and policies for the collection, processing, analysis, presentation, and distribution of statistical data. The full text of the journal (since 1985) is available online: http://www.jos.nu

References

Asiu, B. W., Antons, C. M., and Fultz, M. L. "Undergraduate Perceptions of Survey Participation: Improving Response Rates and Validity." Paper presented at the annual meeting of the Association of Institutional Research, Minneapolis, Minn., May 1998.

Atrostic, B. K., Bates, N., Burt, G., and Silberstein, A. "Nonresponse in U.S. Government Household Surveys: Consistent Measures, Recent Trends, and New Insights." *Journal of Official Statistics,* 2001, *17*(2), 209–226.

Baruch, Y. "Response Rate in Academic Studies: A Comparative Analysis." *Human Relations,* 1999, *52*(4), 421–438.

Berk, M. L., Mathiowetz, N. A., Ward, E. P., and White, A. A. "The Effect of Prepaid and Promised Incentives: Results of a Controlled Experiment." *Journal of Official Statistics,* 1987, *3*(4), 449–457.

Berry, S. H., and Kanouse, D. E. "Physician Response to a Mailed Survey: An Experiment in Timing of Payment." *Public Opinion Quarterly,* 1987, *51*(1), 102–114.

Bogen, K. *The Effect of Questionnaire Length on Response Rates: A Review of the Literature.* Washington, D.C.: U.S. Census Bureau, 1996.

Brehm, J. "Stubbing Out Toes for a Foot in the Door? Prior Contact, Incentives and Survey Response." *International Journal of Public Opinion Research,* 1994, *6*(1), 45–63.

Carini, R. M., Hayek, J. C., Kuh, G. D., Kennedy, J. M., and Ouimet, J. A. "College Student Responses to Web and Paper Surveys: Does Mode Matter?" *Research in Higher Education,* 2003, *44*(1), 1–19.

Church, A. H. "Estimating the Effect of Incentives on Mail Survey Response Rates: A Meta-Analysis. *Public Opinion Quarterly,* 1993, *57,* 62–67.

Cobanoglu, C., Warde, B., and Moreo, P. J. "A Comparison of Mail, Fax and Web-Based Survey Methods." *International Journal of Market Research,* 2001, *43*(4), 441–452.

Cook, C., Heath, F., and Thompson, R. L. "A Meta-Analysis of Response Rates in Web- or Internet-Based Surveys." *Educational and Psychological Measurement,* 2000, *60*(6), 821–836.

Couper, M. P., and Groves, R. M. "Theoretical Motivation for Post-Survey Nonresponse Adjustment in Household Surveys." *Journal of Official Statistics,* 1995, *11*(1), 93–106.

Couper, M. P., and Groves, R. M. "Social Environmental Impacts on Survey Cooperation." *Quality and Quantity,* 1996, *30,* 173–188.

Crawford, S. D., Couper, M. P., and Lamias, M. J. "Web Surveys: Perceptions of Burden." *Social Science Computer Review,* 2001, *19*(2), 146–162.

de Heer, W. "International Response Trends: Results of an International Survey. *Journal of Official Statistics,* 1999, *15*(2), 129–142.

Dey, E. "Working with Low Survey Response Rates: The Efficacy of Weighting Adjustments." *Research in Higher Education,* 1997, *38*(2), 215–227.

Dillman, D. A. "Why Innovation Is Difficult in Government Surveys." *Journal of Official Statistics,* 1996, *12*(2), 113–124.

Dillman, D. A. *Mail and Internet Surveys: The Tailored Design Method.* New York: Wiley, 2000.

Dillman, D. A., and Bowker, D. K. "The Web Questionnaire Challenge to Survey Methodologists." In U.-D. Reips and M. Bosnjak (Eds.), *Dimensions of Internet Science.* Lengerich, Germany: Pabst Science, 2001.

Dillman, D. A., Clark, J. R., and Sinclair, M. D. "How Prenotice Letters, Stamped Return Envelopes and Reminder Postcards Affect Mailback Response Rates for Census Questionnaires." *Survey Methodology,* 1995, *21*(2), 159–165.

Dillman, D. A., Sinclair, M. D., and Clark, J. R. "Effects of Questionnaire Length, Respondent-Friendly Design, and a Difficult Question on Response Rates for Occupant-Addressed Census Mail Surveys." *Public Opinion Quarterly,* 1993, *57*(3), 289–304.

Dillman, D. A., Singer, E., Clark, J. R., and Treat, J. B. "Effects of Benefits Appeals, Mandatory Appeals, and Variations in Statements of Confidentiality on Completion Rates for Census Questionnaires. *Public Opinion Quarterly,* 1996, *60,* 376–389.

Dillman, D. A., Tortora, R. D., Conradt, J., and Bowker, D. K. "Influence of Plain vs. Fancy Design on Response Rates for Web Surveys." Paper presented at the Joint Statistical Meetings, Dallas, Texas, 1998.

Dossett, D. L., Latham, G. O., and Saari, L. M. "The Impact of Goal Setting on Survey Returns." *Academy of Management Journal,* 1980, *23*(3), 561–567.

Fox, R. J., Crask, M. R., and Kim, J. "Mail Survey Response Rate: A Meta-Analysis of Selected Techniques for Inducing Response." *Public Opinion Quarterly,* 1988, *52*(4), 467–491.

Goldstein, K. M., and Jennings, M. K. "The Effect of Advance Letters on Cooperation in a List Sample Telephone Survey." *Public Opinion Quarterly,* 2002, *66*(3), 608–617.

Goyder, J. C. "Further Evidence on Factors Affecting Response Rates to Mailed Questionnaires." *American Sociological Review,* 1982, *47*(4), 550–553.

Goyder, J., Warriner, K., and Miller, S. "Evaluating Socio-Economic Status (SES) Bias in Survey Nonresponse." *Journal of Official Statistics,* 2002, *18*(1), 1–11.

Groves, R. M. *Survey Errors and Survey Costs.* New York: Wiley, 1989.

Groves, R. M., Cialdini, R. B., and Couper, M. P. "Understanding the Decision to Participate in a Survey." *Public Opinion Quarterly,* 1992, *56,* 475–495.

Groves, R. M., Singer, E., and Corning, A. "Leverage-Saliency Theory of Survey Participation." *Public Opinion Quarterly,* 2000, *64,* 299–308.

Groves, R. M., Singer, E., Corning, A. D., and Bowers, A. "A Laboratory Approach to Measuring the Effects on Survey Participation of Interview Length, Incentives, Differential Incentives, and Refusal Conversion." *Journal of Official Statistics,* 1999, *15*(2), 251–268.

Handwerk, P., Carson, C., and Blackwell, K. "On-Line Versus Paper-and-Pencil Surveying of Students: A Case Study." Paper presented at the Association of Institutional Research Conference, Cincinnati, Ohio, May 2000.

Haraldsen, G., Stalnacke, M., and Fosen, J. "Empirical Contributions to a General Survey Response Model." Paper presented at the International Conference on Survey Nonresponse, Portland, Oreg., October 1999.

Heberlein, T. A., and Baumgartner, R. "Factors Affecting Response Rates to Mailed Questionnaires: A Quantitative Analysis of the Published Literature." *American Sociological Review,* 1978, *43*(4), 447–462.

Hox, J., de Leeuw, E., and Vorst, H. "Survey Participation as Reasoned Action: A Behavioral Paradigm for Survey Nonresponse?" *Bulletin de Methodologie Sociologique,* 1995, *48,* 52–67.

James, J. M., and Bolstein, R. "The Effect of Monetary Incentives and Follow-Up Mailings on the Response Rate and Response Quality in Mail Surveys." *Public Opinion Quarterly,* 1990, *54*(3), 346–361.

James, J. M., and Bolstein, R. "Large Monetary Incentives and Their Effect on Mail Survey Response Rates." *Public Opinion Quarterly,* 1992, *56,* 442–453.

Kalton, G. *Introduction to Survey Sampling.* Thousand Oaks, Calif.: Sage, 1983.

Mehta, R., and Sivadas, E. "Comparing Response Rates and Response Content in Mail Versus Electronic Mail Surveys." *Journal of the Market Research Society,* 1995, *37*(4), 429–439.

Mitra, A., Hazen, M. D., LaFrance, B., and Rogan, R. G. "Faculty Use and Non-use of Electronic Mail: Attitudes, Expectations and Profiles." *Journal of Computer Mediated Communication,* 1999, *4*(3), 1–21.

Mowen, J. C., and Cialdini, R. B. "On Implementing the Door-in-the-Face Compliance Technique in a Business Context." *Journal of Marketing Research,* 1980, *17,* 253–258.

Porter, S. R., and Whitcomb, M. E. "The Impact of Contact Type on Web Survey

Response Rates." Paper presented at the North East Association of Institutional Research, Annapolis, Md., November 2002.

Roberts, R. E., McCrory, O. F., and Forthofer, R. N. "Further Evidence on Using a Deadline to Stimulate Responses to a Mail Survey." *Public Opinion Quarterly*, 1978, 42(3), 407–410.

Roscoe, H. S., Terkla, D. G., and Dyer, J. A. "Administering Surveys on the Web: Methodological Issues." Paper presented at the annual conference of the Association of Institutional Research, Toronto, Canada, June 2002.

Schaefer, D. R., and Dillman, D. A. "Development of a Standard E-mail Methodology: Results of an Experiment." *Public Opinion Quarterly*, 1998, 62(3), 378–397.

Schlitz, M. "Professional Standards for Survey Research." *Research in Higher Education*, 1988, 28(1), 67–75.

Shannon, D. M., and Bradshaw, C. C. "A Comparison of Response Rate, Response Time, and Costs of Mail and Electronic Surveys." *Journal of Experimental Education*, 2002, 70(2), 179–192.

Sharp, L. M., and Frankel, J. "Respondent Burden: A Test of Some Common Assumptions." *Public Opinion Quarterly*, 1983, 47(1), 36–53.

Singer, E., Hippler, H.-J., and Schwarz, N. "Confidentiality Assurances in Surveys: Reassurance or Threat?" *International Journal of Public Opinion Research*, 1992, 4, 256–268.

Singer, E., van Hoewyk, J., and Maher, M. P. "Does the Payment of Incentives Create Expectation Effects?" *Public Opinion Quarterly*, 1998, 62, 154–164.

Singer, E., van Hoewyk, J., and Maher, M. P. "Experiments with Incentives in Telephone Surveys." *Public Opinion Quarterly*, 2000, 64, 171–188.

Singer, E., von Thurn, D. R., and Miller, E.R.M. "Confidentiality Assurances and Response: A Quantitative Review of the Experimental Literature." *Public Opinion Quarterly*, 1995, 59, 66–77.

Smith, K., and Bers, T. "Improving Alumni Survey Response Rates: An Experiment and Cost-Benefit Analysis." *Research in Higher Education*, 1987, 27(3), 218–226.

Steeh, C. G. "Trends in Nonresponse Rates, 1952–1979." *Public Opinion Quarterly*, 1981, 59, 66–77.

Warriner, K., Goyder, J., Gjertsen, H., Hohner, P., and McSpurren, K. "Charities, No; Lotteries, No; Cash, Yes." *Public Opinion Quarterly*, 1996, 60, 542–562.

Weible, R., and Wallace, J. "Cyber Research: The Impact of the Internet on Data Collection." *Marketing Research*, 1998, 10(3), 19–23.

Willimack, D. E., Schuman, H., Pennell, B.-E., and Lepkowski, J. M. "Effects of a Prepaid Nonmonetary Incentive on Response Rates and Response Quality in a Face-to-Face Survey." *Public Opinion Quarterly*, 1995, 59, 78–92.

Yammarino, F. J., Skinner, S. J., and Childers, T. L. "Understanding Mail Survey Response Behavior: A Meta-analysis." *Public Opinion Quarterly*, 1991, 55(4), 613–639.

Yu, J., and Cooper, H. "A Quantitative Review of Research Design Effects on Response Rates to Questionnaires." *Journal of Marketing Research*, 1983, 20, 36–44.

STEPHEN R. PORTER *is director of institutional research at Wesleyan University.*

This chapter summarizes the most recent literature on the best practices of Web survey implementation and offers practical advice for researchers.

Web Surveys: Best Practices

Paul D. Umbach

Within four years of its introduction, the Internet was being used by nearly fifty million people worldwide (Cook, Heath, and Thompson, 2000). Reports suggest that approximately fifty-five million Americans went online everyday in 2000. Some researchers have even projected that one billion members of the earth's population will be Web-literate by 2005 (Sheehan and Hoy, 1999). The rapid proliferation of the Internet has resulted in one of the most dramatic changes in survey research in recent years. The ability to collect survey data quickly and inexpensively via the Web seems to have enticed many to launch Web-based surveys.

It now seems as if Web-based surveys are everywhere on the Internet. Their aggressive increase has caused some researchers to suggest that data that at one time were collected by other modes are now being collected by Web surveys (Dillman and Bowker, 2001). It is important, however, for researchers to consider the advantages and disadvantages of Web-based surveys before collecting data. As one might expect, the quality of Web surveys varies tremendously. This chapter reviews the literature on best practices of survey research and provides examples from my own experience using Web-based surveys.

The chapter is organized into three sections. First, I review the literature, highlighting the advantages and disadvantages of Web-based surveys that researchers should consider as they build a survey strategy. Second, I expand the review of the literature to include research on best practices for Web-survey research and ways to increase response rates. Finally, I provide a brief and practical list of issues that researchers should consider while conducting a Web-based survey.

NEW DIRECTIONS FOR INSTITUTIONAL RESEARCH, no. 121, Spring 2004 © Wiley Periodicals, Inc.

Review of the Literature

Although Web surveys are relatively new, the body of research related to them is quite large. In this section, I summarize the relevant research related to the advantages and disadvantages of Web surveys.

Advantages of Web-Based Surveys. One of the greatest advantages of Web-based surveys is that they offer researchers and college administrators a low-cost option for data collection (Carini and others, 2003; Dillman, 2000; Schmidt, 1997; Shannon, Johnson, Searcy, and Lott, 2001; Watt, 1999). One researcher estimated that the total cost for a Web survey of ten thousand people was $.65 per completed survey (Yun and Trumbo, 2000). Postage for the mailing of one paper survey alone can cost $.65, and there is no guarantee of return. Assuming a 50 percent response rate from only one mailing, the paper survey would cost $1.30 per completed survey. The cost per respondent only increases when postage for multiple reminders is included.

Although it is likely that most researchers will save money with Web surveys, they must also consider the human labor costs involved in conducting a Web survey, many of which are difficult to calculate. The costs of building the Web form, managing e-mail addresses, sending invitation and reminder e-mails, and maintaining computer networks cannot be overlooked. As researchers consider the labor costs of Web-based surveys, they should note that the cost per response from a Web survey decreases significantly as sample size increases (Yun and Trumbo, 2000).

In addition to lowering costs, Web-based surveys generally save time. Sending reminders and downloading data are two areas in which researchers can save time by doing a Web survey rather than a mail survey (Gunn, 2002). Probably the greatest time savings is in turnaround time (Berge and Collins, 1996; Schmidt, 1997; Zhang, 1999). A mail survey can take several days to reach an individual and several days to return after completion. Assuming that an individual completes the survey immediately, the process can take a minimum of five to seven days. With Web-based surveys, the invitation reaches the subject almost instantaneously. If an individual chooses to complete the survey, responses are recorded and available for analysis immediately after completion.

Web-based surveys may also reduce errors resulting from coding (Zhang, 1999). In Web-based surveys, responses are already in electronic format and have been coded by the respondent. Few researchers consider the human error in data entry and scanning, both of which are not involved in Web-based data collection. Respondents to Web-based surveys enter their data for the researcher.

Many have suggested that design flexibility is an advantage when conducting Web-based surveys (Dillman, 2000; Zhang, 1999). With relative ease, researchers are able to order questions randomly and offer different questionnaires for different people or groups. Additionally, Web surveys can be more refined in appearance than paper surveys. More important, Web-based surveys can be designed to provide a dynamic survey process by including pop-up instructions, drop-down boxes, and check boxes. Skip patterns can be built in to allow for easy navigation. Some evidence suggests that all of these design advantages may increase a respondent's motivation to complete a survey (Schmidt, 1997; Zhang, 1999).

Research also indicates some social advantages related to Web-based surveys. Some researchers have suggested that students are more likely to answer socially threatening questions when responding to a Web survey (Pealer and others, 2001). In addition, Web-based surveys offer a way to reach a group that normally may be difficult to identify or access, such as gay, lesbian, bisexual, and transgender college students (Coomber, 1997; Zhang, 1999). Other researchers have suggested that surveying via the Web reduces or eliminates social desirability effects (Tourangeau, Couper, and Steiger, 2001).

Finally, Web surveys also have some advantages for data analysis. Researchers have a relatively unlimited scope in determining a sample (Sills and Song, 2002; Zhang, 1999). They can effectively and economically survey an entire population of a particular group rather than a sample, which allows them to reduce or eliminate the effects of sampling error (Sills and Song, 2002). Surveying large numbers of people is also helpful when studying underrepresented groups in a population. Many times researchers are unable to analyze effectively and make claims about a group because they have too few respondents from that group. The ability to survey large numbers of people may ameliorate the problem of small groups.

Disadvantages of Web-Based Surveys. While Web-based surveys have numerous advantages, they also have several disadvantages. When conducting any survey, it is important to consider possible sources of error, ethical issues, and expertise required.

Error. One of the most commonly cited problems with Web-based surveys is error. Researchers (Couper, 2000; Dillman and Bowker, 2001; Dillman, Tortora, and Bowker, 1998) suggest that Web surveys have unique challenges related to bias resulting from coverage error, sampling error, measurement error, and nonresponse error.

Coverage error results from a mismatch between the target population and the frame population. The target population refers to the larger group about which one wishes to make inferences. The frame population is a subset of the population created by limiting the group based on method of access. For example, institutional researchers might determine their target population to be all undergraduates at their institution. The frame population may be all undergraduates who have an accurate e-mail address on record with the institution. When the frame population does not fully "cover" the target population, representativeness is threatened.

Couper (2000) suggests two problems related to coverage in Web-administered surveys. First, not everyone who is in the target population is in the frame population. Using the example just mentioned, not all under-graduates are likely to be included in the researchers' frame population. Before collecting data, they have introduced bias into the study. The second problem is determining the frame for all those included in a Web-based survey. Again, returning to the example, it will be difficult to determine how many students have an active e-mail account that they check on a regular basis. While lack of coverage is likely to decrease as more people become Web literate, it is still one of the biggest threats to the representativeness of Web surveys (Couper, 2000).

Another often-overlooked source of error in Web surveys is *sampling error*. A basic assumption in survey research is that the precision of results for a simple random sample of a defined population is related to sample size. Unless, however, all members of a population are given an equal chance to be included in a sample, the sample, no matter how large, cannot be said to represent the population. Those members of the population who do not have access to the Web cannot have an equal chance of participating in a Web-based survey.

Assuming that no other sources of error are present, sampling error is then largely dependent on the number of people included in the sample. Dillman and Bowker (2001, p. 47) warn, however, that those who conduct Web surveys appear to be "seduced by the hope that large numbers, a traditional indicator of a high quality survey (because of low sampling error), will compensate in some undefined way for whatever coverage and non-response problems that might exist."

Measurement error results from inaccurate responses due to survey mode effects. Some researchers have suggested that mode effects, a form of bias, are a disadvantage of Web surveys. In other words, do Web survey responses differ from paper survey responses? Some researchers have found differences in attitudes between those who responded to a survey on the Web and those who completed a paper-and-pencil version of the survey (Sax, Gilmartin, and Bryant, 2003). As one might expect, research suggests that there are large mode differences on technology-related survey questions. In other words, those who choose to complete a survey online (rather than on paper) tend to be more technologically savvy (Carini and others, 2003).

It also seems that surveying via the Web presents new sources of measurement error. A Web survey can look different depending on a respondent's Web browser, operating system, screen configuration, and hardware (Dillman, 2000; Dillman and Bowker, 2001). Because of these differences, the survey items may appear different from what was intended by the survey designer. The unintended delivery of unequal stimuli introduces the potential for measurement error.

Nonresponse Bias. Another disadvantage of Web-based survey research is an increased likelihood of nonresponse bias. Nonresponse bias is defined as the bias that is introduced when respondents to a survey are different from those who did not respond in terms of demographics or attitudes. The problem arises when individuals in a sample are unwilling or unable to complete a survey. This is particularly problematic for Web-based survey research because individuals may not have equal access to the Web, thereby limiting or preventing them from completing a survey. Studies indicate that certain social groups are underrepresented among Internet users, including people of limited financial resources, members of some racial and ethnic minorities, people at low education levels, and older people (Zhang, 1999). Some researchers have also found response rate differences between men and women (Sax, Gilmartin, and Bryant, 2003).

Nonresponse bias is particularly troubling when response rates are low. While the research on response rates for Web-based surveys is both limited and mixed, several researchers have found that Web-based surveys elicit lower response rates than paper-and-pencil surveys (Crawford, Couper, and Lamias, 2001; Guterbock, Meekins, Weaver, and Fries, 2000; Kwak and Radler, 2000; Sax, Gilmartin, and Bryant, 2003; Tomsic, Hendel, and Matross, 2000; Underwood, Kim, and Matier, 2000). One researcher even reported a response rate of 0 percent (Pradhan, 1999).

Some have suggested that dramatic differences in computer equipment may suppress response rates for Web-based surveys (Dillman, 2000). Out-of-date or inadequate Web browsers may prevent some people from even accessing the survey (Smith, 1997). Additionally, different levels of technical ability may introduce bias (Berge and Collins, 1996; Zhang, 1999).

Ethical Considerations. Web-based surveys are mired in ethical issues not often considered by researchers. Protecting participant privacy and confidentiality is a challenge for researchers conducting Web-based surveys (Cho and LaRose, 1999). Many people consider "spamming," the sending of unwanted e-mails, to be a misuse of technology (Cho and LaRose, 1999; Shannon, Johnson, Searcy, and Lott, 2001). Some even consider mass mailings to large lists of people inviting them to participate in a Web survey to be an invasion of privacy. Reactions to privacy violations on the Web and by e-mail can often be severe because of the limitless boundaries created by the Web. It seems that electronic intrusions violate the privacy of an individual in a way that a letter or a telephone call does not (Cho and LaRose, 1999).

Researchers can also collect information about respondents without their permission, such as the computer's Internet protocol address and how long it took to complete a survey. Can this information be used for research purposes and reported? The answer is not clear. Researchers should tread lightly in this area. The relationship between respondents and their personal computers is a new boundary that researchers should be cautious to cross. The damage done by a few careless researchers can have negative impacts on future Web-based survey research.

An additional ethical concern of Web-based research is data security. To protect the anonymity and confidentiality of respondents, Web researchers are ethically obligated to take every precaution to secure their data. Nevertheless, no one can guarantee the absolute security of Web-based survey data.

Technical Expertise Required. A final disadvantage of Web surveys is the technical expertise required to administer a Web-based survey. Many researchers see this requirement to be far greater than for traditional survey methods (Zhang, 1999). While Web development tools are becoming more user-friendly (for example, ColdFusion and Microsoft FrontPage), researchers hoping to create a Web form need relatively advanced computer knowledge. If they do not have that knowledge or the time to obtain it, they need to rely on a programmer with the skills necessary to build a Web survey.

Best Practices from the Literature

A review of the literature on Web-based surveys may lead many to conclude that the disadvantages far outweigh the advantages. If after weighing the pros and cons of Web-based surveys a research office decides to administer one (see also the discussion in Chapter Seven in this volume), the survey research literature offers a good list of best practices.

The design of Web-based surveys is of greater importance than the design of paper surveys because of the visual emphasis of the Web and the varying appearances between browsers (Couper, 2000). Although experts suggest that design can affect response overall and item nonresponse, most do not advocate any one design format (Couper, Traugott, and Lamas, 2001; Gunn, 2002). The design should reflect the purpose of the survey and should be tailored to the population under study.

Most experts agree, however, that researchers should keep their Web-based survey design simple. Table 2.1 summarizes some of the Web survey design considerations, the type of error each is intended to address, and references where more information can be obtained. Only one of the principles in Table 2.1 addresses sampling error, although somewhat indirectly. Limiting access by the use of a password prevents those who are not in the sample from participating in the survey. This restriction also positively affects coverage. Other principles that deal with coverage are allowing respondents to scroll from question to question, avoiding differences in appearance because of hardware and software differences, and indicating to respondents how much time they have left until they complete the survey, all of which address differences in respondents' technological ability. In addition, respondents are more likely to abandon the survey if they see a counter that reports Web site visits or if long surveys appear on a single page. Web surveys must be easy to navigate, removing any impediment to completion.

Most of these principles address measurement error. Two of them deal with differences in what a programmer intends and what a respondent

Table 2.1. Best Practices for Web Design, Error Addressed, and References

Design Principle	Sampling	Coverage	Measurement	Nonresponse	References
1. Avoid using too much color so that survey is readable and easy to navigate.			X		Dillman, 2000; Dillman and Bowker, 2001; Dillman, Tortora, and Bowker, 1998
2. Provide a password to limiting access to only those people in the sample.	X	X			Crawford, Couper, and Lamias, 2001; Dillman and Bowker, 2001; Dillman, Tortora, and Bowker, 1998; Heerwegh and Loosveldt, 2002
3. Make the first question an item that is interesting, easily answered, and visible on the first screen of the questionnaire.				X	Dillman, 2000; Dillman and Bowker, 2001; Dillman, Tortora, and Bowker, 1998
4. Use a conventional format similar to paper questionnaires.			X	X	Dillman, 2000; Dillman and Bowker, 2001; Dillman, Tortora, and Bowker, 1998
5. Unless order effects are important, allow respondents to scroll from question to question.		X	X	X	Dillman, 2000; Dillman and Bowker, 2001; Dillman, Tortora, and Bowker, 1998
6. Use restraint when including question structures that have known problems on paper surveys (such as open-ended questions and check all that apply).			X	X	Bosnjak and Tuten, 2001; Couper, 2000; Couper, Traugott, and Lamas, 2001; Crawford, Couper, and Lamias, 2001; Dillman, 2000; Dillman and Bowker, 2001
7. Use a welcome screen that is motivating.				X	Couper, 2000; Dillman, 2000; Dillman and Bowker, 2001; Dillman, Tortora, and Bowker, 1998; Gunn, 2002
8. Avoid the use of drop-down boxes.			X		Dillman, 2000; Dillman, Tortora, and Bowker, 1998
9. Limit line length to make it less likely that respondents will skip words.			X	X	Dillman, 2000; Dillman, Tortora, and Bowker, 1998; Gunn, 2002

Table 2.1. (continued) Best Practices for Web Design, Error Addressed, and References

Design Principle	Type of Error				References
	Sampling	Coverage	Measurement	Nonresponse	
10. Provide clear and specific instructions about how to navigate through the survey (for example, skip directions) and how to answer questions.			X	X	Dillman, 2000; Dillman, Tortora, and Bowker, 1998; Gunn, 2002
11. Do not include a counter that measures Web site visits.		X		X	Manfreda, Batagelj, and Vehovar, 2002
12. Test your survey on different computers to avoid differences in the visual appearance resulting from differences in screen configurations, operating systems, and browsers.		X	X	X	Couper, 2000; Couper, Traugott, and Lamas, 2001; Dillman, 2000; Dillman and Bowker, 2001; Dillman, Tortora, and Bowker, 1998
13. Include a progress timer to indicate to respondents approximately how much more time it will take to complete the survey.		X		X	Couper, 2000; Couper, Traugott, and Lamas, 2001; Crawford, Couper, and Lamias, 2001; Dillman and Bowker, 2001; Dillman, Tortora, and Bowker, 1998
14. Do not require answers to each question before allowing respondents to continue with the survey.		X		X	Dillman, 2000; Dillman and Bowker, 2001; Dillman, Tortora, and Bowker, 1998
15. Divide long surveys into sections.		X	X	X	Couper, 2000; Gunn, 2002

Source: Adapted from Dillman and Bowker, 2001.

actually sees on the computer screen. Differences in hardware and software can be reduced by paying attention to use of color and testing the survey on different machines and platforms. Principles 8 and 12 in Table 2.1 are suggestions unique to Web surveys. Drop-down boxes should be used sparingly, and directions, particularly when using links to skip ahead, should be clear. Principles 4 and 5 rely on research from paper surveys and are particularly important when doing a mixed-mode survey (Dillman and Bowker, 2001; Dillman, Tortora, and Bowker, 1998).

Several of the principles also address nonresponse error. All are aimed at reducing possible complications (and resulting frustrations) that can lead to nonresponse. Principle 1 aims at engaging respondents in a way that motivates them to complete the survey. Eliminating the frustrations associated with drop-down boxes, open-ended questions, and unclear skip links are all measures that can reduce nonrespondents' error. Keeping respondents from becoming discouraged by providing them with a progress timer is also important.

Increasing Response Rates

Conspicuously absent from the list of best practices in Table 2.1 are ways to boost response rates in Web-based surveys. This is intentional, because the research on Web survey administration is limited. Much of what Web survey researchers are doing relies heavily on best practices in mail surveys (see Dillman, 2000).

As with mail surveys, Web-based surveys require researchers to provide follow-up reminders. When considering how many times to contact individuals in a sample, one should know that returns drop off almost immediately and at a rapid rate. Some researchers have suggested that if people are going to complete a Web survey, they are going to do so in the first few hours or days (Crawford, Couper, and Lamias, 2001). One study suggests that a single reminder e-mail will double the number of respondents (Crawford, Couper, and Lamias, 2001). The same study found greater returns when the reminder was sent two days after the initial notification e-mail.

How many follow-up e-mails should one send? If no follow up e-mails are sent, one can expect a response rate of less than 30 percent (Cook, Heath, and Thompson, 2000). Some have advocated the use of an initial e-mail notification with two follow-up e-mails (Couper, Traugott, and Lamas, 2001). One study even suggested that four contacts yield the highest response rate (Schaefer and Dillman, 1998). Much of the decision on the number of contacts depends on who is being surveyed. If individuals in the sample are likely to be sensitive to e-mail contacts, then the researcher should reduce the number of e-mails sent.

What format should the e-mail take? Because almost all e-mail programs now accept e-mail in Hypertext Markup Language (HTML) format, researchers have many options in deciding what format to use for their e-mails. As with the Web survey design, research suggests that e-mail formats should be simple (Porter and Whitcomb, 2003). E-mails with nonwhite backgrounds and complex graphic designs may suppress response rates.

Some research indicates that the e-mail content itself is an important way of inducing responses. In mail surveys, individuals can examine the entire survey and decide whether they want to complete it. In Web surveys, this information is not available until the respondent accesses the Web site hosting the survey. Given this difference, the initial letter or e-mail plays an important role in eliciting response (Crawford, Couper, and Lamias, 2001). Some researchers (Crawford, Couper, and Lamias, 2001; Dillman, 2000) offer suggestions about e-mail content, but little is known about the impact of this content. In addition to paying attention to the advice given by the aforementioned experts, one should also pay attention to the content of the contact letter and embed a link to the survey in the text as well as provide an estimate of the time it will take to complete the survey. One study found a boost in response rates if the researcher offered a deadline and included a statement indicating that the respondent was part of a small group chosen to participate in the study (Porter and Whitcomb, forthcoming).

Compared to the importance of cover letters for paper surveys, the importance of personalized e-mails is not entirely clear. A meta-analysis of sixty-eight Web surveys suggests that an e-mail with a personalized salutation does have a positive effect on response rates (Cook, Heath, and Thompson, 2000). However, one recent study found that personalized e-mails, whether using a personalized salutation or a personal e-mail address rather than an office e-mail address, have no effect on response rates (Porter and Whitcomb, forthcoming).

Many researchers have also suggested that survey length plays an important role in response rates. Given the fast-paced nature of the Web, most researchers suggest that surveys should be kept short (Crawford, Couper, and Lamias, 2001; Shannon, Johnson, Searcy, and Lott, 2001). One author recommends that the survey take no longer than ten minutes to complete (Crawford, Couper, and Lamias, 2001). Others suggest keeping the survey length to less than twenty minutes (Gunn, 2002).

As the literature on mail surveys also suggests, the impact of incentives in Web-based surveys is mixed. Some research indicates that incentives have no effect on Web survey response rates (Cook, Heath, and Thompson, 2000; see also Chapter Four, this volume). Other research indicates some increase in response rates when an incentive is introduced (Bosnjak and Tuten, 2001; Couper, 2000; Gunn, 2002; Underwood, Kim, and Matier, 2000).

What conclusions arise from this review of the literature on boosting response rates in Web surveys? First, the area is ripe for research. Research on the impact of the content of e-mail contacts, of the format of e-mail contacts, of the number of contacts, and of incentives on Web survey response rates are among the topics on which more empirical research is needed. Although we know very little about how to increase response rates for Web surveys, the following suggestions are based on limited research cited in this chapter:

- *Use multiple e-mail contacts.* At the very least, send an initial e-mail followed by one reminder. If possible, send one or two additional reminders.
- *Keep e-mail contact format simple.*
- *The content of the e-mail contacts should be similar to that for a paper survey* (see Dillman, 2000). Be sure, however, to include a deadline and inform the respondent how long it will take to complete the survey. Also, indicate that the recipient is one of a small group selected for the study.
- *Personalize the e-mail letters.* Although studies on the effect of the personalization of e-mails are mixed, current software packages make it relatively easy to personalize e-mails.
- *Keep the survey short, no longer than twenty minutes.* Pilot test the survey for a clear understanding of how long it takes to complete.
- *Do not feel pressure to offer an incentive to survey respondents.* If you can afford incentives (which most researchers cannot) or have them donated, feel free to include them. Then offer the incentive to half the group to see if their response rate differs from that of the group that did not receive an incentive.

Best Practices from Survey Experience

Based on my own experiences with Web surveys of students, alumni, college faculty, and senior administrators, I offer some additional best practices for Web-based survey implementation.

Know All of Your Costs. Although doing a Web survey is economical, it is important to know the hidden costs, often in your time, of conducting a Web survey. If you do not have a programmer to build your Web form and do not have the appropriate programming experience, it will probably take you twice as long as you expect to prepare the survey. If you rely on programmers, you also need to calculate the costs of their time.

On one occasion I did not have the assistance of a programmer and was forced to build the page myself. While the latest software makes programming Web pages relatively easy, all of them require some writing of code to maximize the functionality of Web data collection. After more than forty hours of programming, I had a functioning Web-based survey.

Your time or your staff members' time commitments do not end with the posting of the survey. Testing the survey and closely examining the data from these tests take time. A few years ago I had a programmer build my Web survey and had several colleagues test it. I took a cursory glance at the data from the tests and went live with the survey. After a week of data collection I requested a data file. I conducted a thorough analysis of the data and found that two of the variables had been given the same name in the programming code. We quickly took down the survey, corrected it, and threw out all of the data collected prior to the correction. Be sure to allocate an adequate amount of time for checking.

Managing bad e-mail addresses, removing respondents from reminder lists, and answering questions may take hours. E-mails from respondents with questions and comments must all get responses in a timely manner. Expect that approximately 10 percent of your target sample will ask questions about the survey.

More May Be More. After you build the Web form and develop a system for managing e-mails, the monetary costs of doing a Web survey are relatively stable regardless of your sample size. So why not survey all of your first-year students rather than sample them? Your sampling error will drop and you might get enough data to do analyses on subgroups (such as colleges or departments) within your institution. Although you are reducing sampling error, keep in mind the other sources of error (nonresponse, coverage, and measurement). You may have ten thousand respondents and still have bias due to other types of error.

Know Who You Are Surveying. One of the most important things to consider when doing a Web survey is who you are surveying. Is it likely that my sample has access to computers and the Web? More and more people are regularly accessing the Web, but some groups are not. In addition to access, consider the computer literacy of your sample. Fortunately for those studying college students, nearly every college student (86 percent) has gone online (Jones, 2002). College faculty or college administrators are not nearly as computer savvy as their students. Recently I worked on a Web-based survey of faculty that yielded approximately three times as many phone calls and e-mails regarding technical problems than a parallel study of college students.

Do the individuals you are surveying have good e-mail addresses that are checked often? Some colleges and universities do not collect e-mail addresses from their students. Do you collect more than one e-mail address? Many colleges assign an e-mail address to every student, but in many cases students do not check these e-mails. Colleges that collect more than one e-mail address may capture more students by sending e-mails to every address on record for each student.

Presample Your Population. If you are uncertain about your population's interest in and responsiveness to a Web-based survey, test the survey on a small sample of the population (Shannon, Johnson, Searcy, and Lott, 2001). Pay close attention to the best practices listed earlier before collecting data. After collecting data from your presample, check for differences in respondent characteristics. If you get an acceptable response rate and the respondents approximate the population, you may have some indication that a Web-based survey will be successful.

Mixed-Mode Administration. Mixed-mode administration may be the answer to low response rates. Some researchers have argued that mixed-mode survey administration may be a way to increase response rates and overcome nonresponse bias and coverage error (Schaefer and Dillman, 1998; Yun and Trumbo, 2000). Researchers might consider starting with an e-mail invitation to participate in a Web-based survey and then move to a paper mailing to nonrespondents. Offering two modes may increase motivation to respond because people appreciate the opportunity to choose their mode (Dillman, 2000). While you might reduce the likelihood of some error, you might also increase the chance of measurement error due to the mode effect. If you chose to use a mixed-mode method, be sure to test for differences in responses due to mode of response.

My personal experiences with mixed-mode administration have been very positive. For my dissertation (Umbach, 2002) I conducted a survey of twenty-seven hundred college deans and vice presidents. I began by sending an e-mail inviting them to participate in the survey. After sending two reminder e-mails, I had more than twelve hundred responses. I then mailed a paper version of the survey to nonrespondents and received more than four hundred responses via the mail. Almost seventeen hundred senior administrators responded to the survey, giving me a response rate of 61 percent. I tested for mode effects and found no significant differences. The total cost for the survey was less than $3,000.

Seek Approval from Your Campus Human Subjects Committee. Not all universities require administrative surveys done by institutional research offices to be approved by a human subjects committee. However, given the ethical considerations discussed earlier in the chapter, seeking such approval is highly recommended. Although the process of obtaining approval can be challenging, the committee can be considered a resource that is there to protect the researcher and the institution.

Take the Pulse of the Group. Perhaps the best use of a Web-based survey is to take the pulse of a group. A short five- to ten-question survey that seeks to obtain the opinion of students, faculty, or staff can be quite useful. One of my first experiences with Web-based surveys was a short survey intended to gain understanding of how faculty and students felt about a proposed new grading system. In coordination with the registrar's office, students were sent a five-question survey after registering for classes via the Web. At the same time we sent an e-mail (and e-mail reminders) to faculty that included a link to a similar survey. In less than three weeks we were able to survey thousands of students and faculty, analyze our results, and present a report to the campus community. In the end the change in policy was not approved, in part because of the information gleaned from our survey.

Conclusion

While this chapter highlights several important issues to consider when conducting a Web-based survey, please note that it has not covered everything you need to know about conducting a good survey. In particular, we have not discussed the survey design principles that apply to all survey research—for example, the principles of good question writing that apply to surveys. For this and other survey design considerations, see the well-known books by Dillman (2000), Salant and Dillman (1994), Converse and Presser (1986), Fowler (1995), and Rea and Parker (1997).

In conclusion, I offer an additional cautionary note. Web-based surveys are relatively new and rapidly evolving. What was considered a best practice a year ago may no longer be a best practice a year from now. This chapter does not provide all of the answers, but it offers a brief review of the current best practices with the hope that you will consider how best to conduct your own survey. I write not as a proponent of any one method of survey administration, but as someone who seeks to find the best method for the research questions asked. Prior to beginning your next survey, please contemplate the advantages and disadvantages of conducting a Web-based survey. If you decide to survey via the Web, think about issues of error and ways to reduce it. Also, consider methods proven to increase response rates. Careful consideration of these issues will make your survey a better one.

References

Berge, Z. L., and Collins, M. P. "IPCT Journal: Readership Survey." *Journal of American Society for Information Science,* 1996, 47(9), 701–710.

Bosnjak, M., and Tuten, T. L. "Classifying Response Behaviors in Web-Based Surveys." *Journal of Computer Mediated Communication,* 2001, 6(3). [http://www.ascusc.org/jcmc/vol6/issue3/boznjak.html]. Access date: Jan. 21, 2004.

Carini, R. M., Hayek, J. C., Kuh, G. D., Kennedy, J. M., and Ouimet, J. A. "College Student Responses to Web and Paper Surveys: Does Mode Matter?" *Research in Higher Education,* 2003, 44(1), 1–19.

Cho, H., and LaRose, R. "Privacy Issues in Internet Surveys." *Social Science Computer Review,* 1999, 17(4), 421–434.

Converse, J. M., and Presser, S. *Survey questions: Handcrafting the standardized questionnaire.* Thousand Oaks, Calif.: Sage, 1986.

Cook, C., Heath, F., and Thompson, R. L. "A Meta-analysis of Response Rates in Web- or Internet-Based Surveys." *Educational and Psychological Measurement,* 2000, 60(6), 821–836.

Coomber, R. "Using the Internet for Survey Research. *Sociological Research Online,* 1997, 2(2). [http://www.socresonline.org.uk/2/2/2.html]. Access date: Jan. 21, 2004.

Couper, M. P. "Web Surveys: A Review of Issues and Approaches." *Public Opinion Quarterly,* 2000, 64, 464–494.

Couper, M. P., Traugott, M. W., and Lamas, M. J. "Web Survey Design and Administration." *Public Opinion Quarterly,* 2001, 65, 230–253.

Crawford, S. D., Couper, M. P., and Lamias, M. J. "Web Surveys: Perceptions of Burden." *Social Science Computer Review,* 2001, 19(2), 146–162.

Dillman, D. A. *Mail and Internet Surveys: The Tailor Design Method.* (2nd ed.) New York: Wiley, 2000.

Dillman, D. A., and Bowker, D. "The Web Questionnaire Challenge to Survey Methodologists." In U.-D. Reips and M. Bosnjak (eds.), *Dimensions of Internet Science.* Lengerich, Germany: Pabst Science, 2001.

Dillman, D. A., Tortora, R. D., and Bowker, D. *Principles for Constructing Web Surveys: An Initial Statement.* (Technical Report 98–50) Pullman, Wash.: Social and Economic Sciences Research Center, Washington State University, 1998.

Fowler, F. J. *Improving Survey Questions: Design and Evaluation.* Thousand Oaks, Calif.: Sage, 1995.

Gunn, H. "Web-Based Surveys: Changing the Survey Process." *First Monday,* 2002, 7(12). [http://www.firstmonday.dk/issues/issue7_12/gunn]. Access date: Jan. 21, 2004.

Guterbock, T. M., Meekins, B. J., Weaver, A. C., and Fries, J. C. "Web Versus Paper: A Mode Experiment in a Survey of University Computing." Paper presented at the annual meeting of the American Association for Public Opinion Research, Portland, Oreg., May 2000.

Heerwegh, D., and Loosveldt, G. "Web Surveys: The Effect of Controlling Survey Access Using PIN Numbers." *Social Science Computer Review,* 2002, 20(1), 10–21.

Jones, S. "The Internet Goes to College: How Students are Living in the Future with Today's Technology." Washington, D.C.: The Pew Internet and American Life Project, 2002. [http://www.pewinternet.org/reports/toc.asp?Report=71]. Access date: Jan. 21, 2004.

Kwak, N., and Radler, B. T. "Using the Web for Public Opinion Research: A Comparative Analysis Between Data Collected via Mail and the Web." Paper presented at the annual meeting of the American Association for Public Opinion Research, Portland, Oreg.: May 2000.

Manfreda, K. L., Batagelj, Z., and Vehovar, V. "Design of Web Survey Questionnaires: Three Basic Experiments." *Journal of Computer Mediated Communication,* 2002, 7(2).

Pealer, L. N., Weiler, R. M., Pigg, R. M., Miller, D., and Dorman, S. M. "The Feasibility of a Web-Based Surveillance System to Collect Health Risk Behavior Data from College Students. *Health Education and Behavior,* 2001, 28(5), 547–599.

Porter, S. R., and Whitcomb, M. E. "The Impact of Contact Type on Web Survey Response Rates." *Public Opinion Quarterly,* forthcoming.

Porter, S. R., and Whitcomb, M. E. "The Impact of Lottery Incentives on Survey Response Rates." *Research in Higher Education,* 2003, 44(4), 389–407.

Pradhan, K. "The Internet in Nepal: A Survey Report." *The International Information and Library Review,* 1999, 31, 41–47.

Rea, L. M., and Parker, R. A. *Designing and Conducting Survey Research: A Comprehensive Guide.* (2nd ed.) San Francisco: Jossey-Bass, 1997.

Salant, P., and Dillman, D. A. *How to Conduct Your Own Survey.* New York: Wiley, 1994.

Sax, L. J., Gilmartin, S. K., and Bryant, A. N. "Assessing Response Rates and Nonresponse Bias in Web and Paper Surveys." *Research in Higher Education,* 2003, 44(4), 409–431.

Schaefer, D. R., and Dillman, D. A. "Development of Standard Email Methodology." *Public Opinion Quarterly,* 1998, 62(3), 378–397.

Schmidt, W. C. "World Wide Web Survey Research: Benefits, Potential Problems, and Solutions." *Behavioral Research Methods, Instruments, and Computers,* 1997, 29, 274–279.

Shannon, D. M., Johnson, T. E., Searcy, S., and Lott, A. "Using Electronic Surveys: Advice from Professionals." *Practical Assessment, Research and Evaluation,* 2001, 8(2). [http://pareonline.net/getvn.asp?v=8&n=1]. Access date: Jan. 21, 2004.

Sheehan, K. B., and Hoy, M. G. "Using Email to Survey Internet Users in the United States: Methodology and Assessment." *Journal of Computer Mediated Communication,* 1999, 43(1).

Sills, S. J., and Song, C. "Innovations in Survey Research: An Application of Web-Based Surveys." *Social Science Computer Review,* 2002, *20*(1), 22–30.

Smith, C. B. "Casting the Net: Surveying an Internet Population." *Journal of Computer Mediated Communication,* 1997, *3,* 77–84.

Tomsic, M. L., Hendel, D. D., and Matross, R. P. "A World Wide Web Response to Student Satisfaction Surveys: Comparisons Using Paper and Internet Formats." Paper presented at the fortieth annual meeting of the Association for Institutional Research, Cincinnati, Ohio, May 2000.

Tourangeau, R., Couper, M. P., and Steiger, D. M. "Social Presence in Web Surveys." Paper presented at the 2001 Federal Committee on Statistical Methodology Conference, Arlington, Virginia, Nov. 14–16, 2001.

Umbach, P. D. *Who Wants to Be a College President? Forms of Capital and the Career Aspirations of Senior College Administrators.* College Park: University of Maryland, 2002.

Underwood, D., Kim, H., and Matier, M. "To Mail or to Web: Comparisons of Survey Response Rates and Respondent Characteristics." Paper presented at the Annual Forum of the Association for Institutional Research, Cincinnati, Ohio, May 2000.

Watt, J. H. "Internet Systems for Evaluation Research." In G. Gay and T. L. Bennington (eds.), *Information Technologies in Evaluation: Social, Moral, Epistemological, and Practical Implications.* San Francisco: Jossey-Bass, 1999.

Whitcomb, M. E., and Porter, S. R. "Email Contacts: A Test of Complex Graphical Designs." Paper presented at the annual meeting of the Northeast Association for Institutional Research, Newport, R.I., Nov. 2003.

Yun, G. W., and Trumbo, C. W. "Comparative Response to a Survey Executed by Post, E-mail, and Web Form." *Journal of Computer Mediated Communication,* 2000, *6*(1).

Zhang, Y. "Using the Internet for Survey Research: A Case Study." *Journal of the American Society for Information Science,* 1999, *51*(1), 57–68.

PAUL D. UMBACH *is project manager and research analyst at the Center for Postsecondary Research at Indiana University.*

3

Many institutions are surveying students about sensitive topics such as alcohol and drug use, sexual behavior, and academic dishonesty. Yet these can be some of the most difficult surveys to administer successfully, given reluctance on the part of respondents both to participate and to provide truthful answers.

Conducting Surveys on Sensitive Topics

John H. Pryor

In an institutional research setting, surveys are often used to uncover information that will assist in decision making. Many times we investigate issues via surveys that include questions one also might ask personally of any college student, such as year in school, varsity sport participation, or hours spent studying. In many cases the responses to these types of questions are not particularly troublesome. Respondents are not particularly concerned if someone can identify their answers, nor are school officials particularly concerned about how the data will reflect on their institution.

There are instances, however, in which institutions need to gather data that are seen as sensitive. Data concerning behavioral issues, such as alcohol and other drug use and sexual behavior, can be used to help pinpoint areas where educational resources are most sorely needed. Such data can also be used to demonstrate progress (or lack thereof) in reducing the impact of such behaviors on academic and social behaviors. But because these data can describe illegal behaviors, violations of school policy, or socially undesirable traits, they are seen as addressing sensitive topics. Surveys of sensitive topics are a special case of surveying, and this chapter illustrates some of the unique considerations that researchers should be aware of when examining such topics.

Types of Sensitivities

Various kinds of sensitivities might arise with respect to survey data. Primarily, sensitivity is present when there is reason to suspect that an individual's responses to a particular question, if disclosed, might put the respondent at risk. It is important to emphasize that this risk need not be great. It might range from a risk of feeling uncomfortable, on the one hand, to being put at risk for criminal prosecution, on the other. A student under the legal age to consume alcohol responding to a question about alcohol use is one example of a sensitive situation, because a response indicating use also admits illegal behavior and a possible violation of school policy. Determining the level of risk, the relative importance of obtaining the responses, and the subsequent level of protection necessary are some of the primary reasons behind the protocols for the protection of human subjects (National Commission for the Protection of Human Subjects of Biomedical and Behavioral Research, 1979).

Sensitivity is also a concern when, regardless of what might or might not happen with the results, merely asking the question raises a concern with the respondent. This is most often encountered in research using questions that can have psychological implications. For instance, a woman answering a questionnaire about rape might encounter questions that recall a personal experience with a sexual assault, which might in turn trigger psychological distress.

In addition, questions that can be viewed as invading the privacy of the respondent can be seen as sensitive (Tourangeau and Smith, 1996). Questions about sexual behavior can be seen as intrusive, whether they evoke positive or negative aspects of such behaviors. For some survey respondents, identification of racial identity is a sensitive topic that some researchers view as "just a demographic" and not sensitive at all.

What should be clear from these examples is that there is a large gray area when determining what a sensitive topic is, and this gray area will vary as a function of the population as well as by individual. What is sensitive for one person is not necessarily sensitive for another.

There are also areas of sensitivity that are particular to institutional research. A survey is a public endeavor. As soon as participants see the questionnaire, it is assumed that the endeavor becomes public knowledge, and with that public knowledge can come public questions. An enterprising college newspaper reporter will want to know why the institution is surveying students about the topic: Do we have a problem with [cheating, alcohol use, diversity] here on campus? It is not just the respondent's view of sensitive topics that must be taken into account, but also the public's view of the asking of such questions and of what the asking implies.

Another area of sensitivity that institutional researchers should keep in mind is one that comes into play when the survey results are collected and examined. Given the public process of surveying just described, the public will know that such questions are being asked and that presumably the answers have been obtained. College officials should expect to be asked about the results and what they imply. If the institution is unprepared or unwilling to tackle the discussion that might be required after obtaining such information, those conducting the assessment might wish they had never asked the questions in the first place. A religiously affiliated university might be challenged by a health survey that reveals sexual practices among the study body that run counter to the stated beliefs of the church and the institution. A woman's college might be apprehensive about data enumerating the same-sex experiences of its undergraduates. Depending on where the institution is situated in considering such questions, the administration, faculty, students, and alumni might or might not welcome the opportunity for dialogue offered by such information. This category of sensitivity is one that requires knowledge of local issues and will likely be different for every institution.

Why Surveys of Sensitive Topics Are Important

Given these caveats, why even conduct such surveys? This is a question that many schools will struggle with when first contemplating such an endeavor. As touched on earlier, there are multiple benefits to conducting such surveys. They gather information that can be used to inform and improve the experiences of the students, faculty, and administration at the institution. For instance, knowing which students are more at risk for health-related alcohol problems can help the administration target prevention and education programs toward those student groups (Pryor and Keeling, 2002). Conducting such assessments over time allows the institution to monitor progress in addressing such issues.

Sensitive topics are rarely encountered when a survey is only being contemplated. It is usually after years of discussion and debate on campus that such an assessment is undertaken. Until such data are obtained, the prevailing descriptions of the problem will usually come in the form of rumors or personal anecdotes. A survey provides another source of information that is more encompassing and standardized. Finally, another consideration is that merely conducting such a survey can send a message that the institution knows that the issue is of concern and is contemplating action.

Concerns About Sensitive-Topic Surveys

A major concern about sensitive-topic surveys is whether or not the responses adequately reflect reality. The underlying assumption here is that respondents will answer nonsensitive questions truthfully because there are no foreseeable negative consequences of admitting their true experiences, beliefs, attitudes, or perceptions relative to such questions. The corollary of this assumption is that when there are foreseeable negative consequences of such admissions, respondents will be motivated to respond less truthfully. Given that different people view different questions as sensitive or not, is it possible to predict response validity without first assessing individual sensitivity? Research on sensitive topics provides some insight into these matters.

If the major impetus to fabricate results is concern about being identified, then the greater the appearance that respondents will be protected
from identification, the greater will be the respondents' propensity toward
telling the truth. It is certain that the methods of surveying can impact the
results that are obtained. One finding from both alcohol and drug research
and research on sexual behavior is that respondents report a greater number of behavioral incidents when using a self-administered questionnaire
than they do in an interview situation (Turner, Lessler, and Gfroerer,
1992; Tourangeau and Smith, 1996; Aquilino, 1994). Social desirability is
assumed to be one mediating factor in decreasing reports of such behaviors. Another factor is the apparent lack of anonymity when actually face-
to-face with an interviewer (Tourangeau and Smith, 1996). The point,
however, that face-to-face interviews are less valid than self-report questionnaires because of the higher level of reporting such behaviors on the
latter assumes that the higher level of reporting is accurate. While "higher
is better" has been assumed when comparing the results obtained by different methodologies, no collection method can claim validity on these
grounds.

More compelling validation studies on alcohol and other drug use
involve comparing self-report data with subsequent (and unforeseen) drug
testing. This line of research demonstrates that respondents who are asked
to complete a self-report survey and then subsequently are asked for a urine
or blood sample to verify the responses are answering the questionnaires
truthfully (Marquis, Marquis, and Polich, 1986; Harrison, 1997). Most
validity testing of self-report measures in this field, however, has been conducted on special populations such as patients in drug treatment or people
in the criminal justice system, so the results might not generalize to other
populations (Harrison, 1997). That most validation studies using medical
testing are comparing against self-reports and not interviews does lend cre-
dence to the supposition that self-reports will be more accurate and that the
higher levels of use obtained under those circumstances are indeed more
likely to reflect reality.

Confidentiality and Anonymity. As mentioned earlier, one of the
factors cited in reduced reporting in interview situations is that anonymity
is less evident in an interview situation. Thus another major concern
related to veracity of the data is how respondents perceive the likelihood
of being personally identified with their answers. Making the process as
protective as possible, and letting participants know this, can help assure
participants that their responses will not come back to haunt them, thus
increasing both potential compliance with the project and the veracity of
the data.

Research on the relative effects of confidentiality versus anonymity has
found mixed results (Durant, Carey, and Schroder, 2002). In some cases no
differences in prevalence have been found, in other cases numbers have
been higher in confidential situations, and in some cases higher percentages

have been found under anonymous conditions. In a variety of experimental conditions, Durant, Carey, and Schroder (2002) demonstrated that one of the more interesting aspects of confidential versus anonymous questionnaires is that an anonymous administration results in a slightly lower prevalence of incomplete responses. This is one compelling argument for anonymous administration, but a recent finding that requires further research.

Issues in Choosing an Instrument. There are two primary ways in which an institution may become involved in surveying on a sensitive topic. First, an individual, group, or several individuals or groups may decide that more information on the topic is necessary, and a survey is at least one of the tools they may employ. Once they have established the need, they will need an instrument. The second way an institution may become involved in surveying a sensitive topic is in a sense the opposite procedure: an individual or a group has an instrument and the institution is approached to participate in the study. The invitation may come from a researcher looking for an institution to participate in a project, from a consortium to which the institution belongs, or from a private group looking to market its services. In these cases, external political issues might impact participation either positively or negatively.

There are many issues to examine when determining how to proceed in choosing an instrument. We first consider the situation in which a group on campus has defined a need to survey and seeks how to best meet that need.

First and foremost, informational needs must be closely examined. This can often be a lengthy process because it requires dialogue between the people who know the most about the issue and researchers who can best identify how to obtain the answers. At this point three questions are on the table: (1) What do we already know about the issue from previous surveys that have asked related questions? (2) How have other institutions investigated this issue? and (3) Should we create our own instrument? Mining previous surveys or institutional data is a good first step, but not one that needs special instructions for sensitive topics.

A good second step is to investigate what other institutions have done under similar circumstances. Three pieces of information are particularly important here: how the survey was administered, what instrument was used, and whether or not the process and results were helpful.

An additional concern is whether to use an already existing instrument or create your own. One of the best reasons to consider an already available instrument is that very often comparative data are available. This is especially important for surveys about sensitive topics because when the results come in people will want a benchmark to help them interpret the results as being better or worse than the results obtained at other institutions. If previous research in the field has established a particular benchmark (such as for binge drinking in alcohol consumption), then an institution should anticipate being asked by various constituents to address this benchmark with any instrument chosen. As one might expect, using sensitive data from other institutions usually requires some caveats, such as not being able to see data in other than an aggregate form and perhaps not being able to openly identify the institutions that are included in the aggregate figures. Nationally available surveys usually have these details spelled out and require a signed statement of willingness to conform to their policies (this protects the institution seeking to use the survey as well). If comparative data are especially important, verify that they will actually be available in the necessary format when needed.

A nationally available instrument that examines sensitive topics will likely have been through several test phases and have reliability and validity data, which might be cumbersome to collect when designing an instrument. Sensitive topics can also have particular nuances that might not be detected until after careful testing which is another reason to investigate available instruments. (Table 3.1 lists several large-scale survey instruments developed to examine sensitive topics that are available for use by institutions of higher education.)

Certainly the instrument that will fit an institution best is one that is carefully crafted for the institution's particular needs. Local jargon can be utilized, making the project seem more knowledgeable (and perhaps then more credible) to the respondents than a formula survey would be. If a campus does not have fraternities or sororities, for instance, then using a pre-existing instrument that contains questions about fraternity drinking might be seen by some potential respondents as illustrating a lack of understanding of the campus's issues.

Creating a questionnaire can be a lengthy and painstaking process, however. As many researchers who have been in this position know, this requires a good deal of patience and education among all participants if the process is to create a satisfactory product. Creating a questionnaire can help create buy-in for the responders (see next section), but because data comparability is lessened, there is less of a context in which to interpret the results.

Stakeholder Buy-in

Regardless of which instrument is used, great care must be given to obtain stakeholder buy-in up front. If an instrument is chosen without careful consideration of what the responses would mean, the survey might be an exercise in futility. Surveys on sensitive topics produce sensitive findings. The institution must be prepared to deal with the findings in some fashion. Having buy-in from the stakeholders as to the importance of the questions before they are asked and answered can lessen the possibility that the findings will be dismissed. Making sure that those who will be affected by the results agree on the importance of asking the questions will increase

Table 3.1. Resources for Surveying Students on Sensitive Topics

Instrument	Source	Topics	URL
Academic Integrity Survey	Center for Academic Integrity	Academic integrity/ cheating	http://www.academicintegrity.org/assessGuide.asp
TheHealthSurvey	Outside the Classroom	Alcohol, tobacco, drugs Sex Eating Suicide Violence and safety Use of health education and counseling	http://www.outsidetheclassroom.com/products/thehealthsurvey.asp
National College Health Assessment	American College Health Association	Alcohol, tobacco, drugs Sex Eating Suicide Violence and safety Vaccinations	http://www.acha.org/projects_programs/assessment.cfm
Core Alcohol and Drug Survey	Core Institute	Alcohol and drugs	http://www.siuc.edu/coreinst

the likelihood of the results being accepted rather than rejected. Sensitive findings are usually uncomfortable for someone. Some people, when confronted with an uncomfortable finding, will attempt to somehow discredit the assessment. One way to discredit the finding is to attack the question as being either flawed or irrelevant. Another way that people can react to findings they perceive as threatening or disturbing is to attack the methodology used in conducting the study. If one has obtained buy-in up front from stakeholders, the chances of countering this argument are increased.

Methodological Concerns

As stated earlier, the methodology used in conducting the survey is likely to be attacked by those who are looking for a way to discredit the results. This is one very good reason for making sure that the methodology is sound. More important is that respondents should be protected from sensitive results being in any way revealed on an individual basis.

Protection of Human Subjects. Although institutions differ in both policy and practice as to whether or not institutional research projects are required to undergo institutional review board approval, surveys of sensitive topics should always go through this process. This offers protection for everyone: the researcher, the institution, and the participants.

Although institutional review boards do not all have the same rules for reviewing research on human subjects, there are some general guidelines that can streamline the process. In recent years compliance with federal regulations has come under increased scrutiny (Gunsalus, 2002), and some institutions have required that all those who submit proposals for review must also have completed a course on the protection of human subjects. Preparing and submitting the materials, as well as waiting for the decision of the review board, can be time-consuming, and this time must be factored into the research schedule. If there are revisions to be made that require a resubmission, this will take further time to accomplish. Although submitting the research plan to a review board is an added burden on the institutional research office, many institutions require all research to be submitted to the review board. Doing so will both comply with institutional regulations and help ensure that the study's methodology protects all the relevant parties in the best way possible.

There are traditionally three levels of human subject review: exempt, expedited, and full review. One error that can be made is for a research office to think that it can determine at which level a particular project belongs. It cannot. The review board has the mandate to make that determination, and one must submit to the board the proper materials for review before it can be determined what level is appropriate for a project. In general a project will qualify as exempt from further review if anonymity is given to the respondents and if the material being examined is not sensitive. If a project is not anonymous—that is, if the data can be linked somehow to the participants—then the project will not likely be considered exempt but may be considered expedited. Usually surveys of sensitive topics will also be considered expedited. Most survey projects do not make it to the next level, full review, which is more often used for medical research that contains a certain level of psychological or physical risk.

Under expedited review, the reviewers will likely be looking for several key criteria to be met. First, if the project is not anonymous, confidentiality should be assured. In many cases, in order to increase response rates, researchers will want to know if a specific individual returned a survey or if he or she needs to be sent a follow-up reminder. This can be difficult to accomplish under conditions of anonymity, so many researchers choose to promise confidentiality instead. Most review boards will want to see a layer of protection for the respondents where the data are kept, such as not having any individually identifiable data present in the response database. In this case, having two databases assists in keeping confidentiality while also allowing respondent status to be tracked: one database contains the identifying factor (name, student identification number, and so on) and a randomly generated identification number, while the database with the survey responses contains only the randomly generated identification number for linkage to the identifying information.

Second, review boards might be concerned if a respondent pool contains people under the age of eighteen and might require special consideration for that group, such as active parental consent.

Third, the review board will want to see all information that is being sent to potential respondents, including any cover letters and the survey instrument itself. Here again review boards differ with respect to the emphases that are placed on certain issues, but in general they will want to see that the project is accurately described to the participant (including who is conducting the research), that anonymity or confidentiality (whichever is appropriate) is explained, that participants are told they have a right to refuse to participate, and that refusal to participate will have no negative repercussions.

Confidentiality and Anonymity. One additional aspect, discussed briefly already, is relevant to sensitive surveys. Those who are asked to participate in the survey will likely not know the difference between confidentiality and anonymity or confuse one with the other. Briefly explaining what is being promised will both educate respondents sufficiently for purposes of human subjects review and anticipate potential questions. Oftentimes simply explaining that the survey is confidential (but not how confidentiality differs from anonymity) will elicit questions later in the survey process. For example, respondents who confuse confidentiality with anonymity may question how anyone knew they had not responded to the first questionnaire or how a prize was awarded for participating. Addressing this issue up front may reduce the number of questions asked as well as increase the response rate.

Respondents are concerned with anonymity and confidentiality in their responses to questions about sensitive topics when they are concerned about the possibility of their individual answers being revealed. Making the process as protective as possible and letting participants know this can help assure them that their responses will not come back to haunt them, and thus increase potential compliance with the project as well as veracity of the data.

Another way to increase the credibility of project safeguards is to provide externally validated assurances concerning the process. One easy way to do this is to provide evidence of permission from the institutional human subjects review board. Another way is to include a letter from an institutional authority figure assuring that the institution will not attempt to identify individuals based on survey data. For instance, a survey on Academic Integrity might include a letter from the dean of students promising that no disciplinary action will occur as a result of survey findings. Finally, there are some federal agencies that provide such verifications. The National Institute on Alcohol Abuse and Alcoholism will provide a "certificate of confidentiality" to research projects that meet their criteria (National Institute of Alcohol Abuse and Alcoholism, 2002). This certificate protects the institution from being legally obligated to provide information obtained from individuals in the course of a research project.

Timing of Your Survey. If a questionnaire asks about sensitive behaviors in order to determine their prevalence over a certain period, it is important to know whether or not the specified period will capture customary behavior or irregular behavior. If an institution is interested in the average amount of alcohol consumed by students, the school calendar should be considered when administering the survey. Administering the survey on the day after spring break ends will gather data about spring break, not about regular college-based behavior. The same caveat applies to large party weekends, when students tend to drink more than average. Not only will conducting a survey at this time produce data that might be misinterpreted, but students will connect the timing with the request and question the veracity of any claims made via the results.

Reporting Issues. Asking questions about sensitive issues is one thing; reporting on them is another. To avoid misunderstandings, specifics about reporting should be considered before gathering the data. In some cases, restrictions concerning reporting might need to be determined before embarking on the project. An institution might agree to participate in a study only if results are to be communicated only to senior officers, for instance. It is usually helpful to have discussions about the findings with stakeholders before any documents are written about the results. This is helpful both from the standpoint of gaining additional perspectives on the issues to be elaborated upon in a report and from the standpoint of needing to give the stakeholders time to make any necessary institutional prepar-ations to address the findings publicly. It is also helpful to coordinate announcements of survey findings with news or public affairs personnel. Sensitive topics can be of great interest to the media, and it helps to have professional media handlers on one's side.

Concluding Remarks

Special circumstances exist when surveys of sensitive topics are considered. While every institutional research project should be carried out with deliberation, surveys of sensitive topics require that even greater care be taken. Such research projects can be of great benefit to an institution, both in dispelling myths where they exist and in helping to determine areas of greatest need. While they are more difficult to manage, surveys of sensitive topics have potential for great payoff in institutional discovery and change.

References

Aquilino, W. "Interview Mode Effects in Surveys of Drug and Alcohol Use: A Field Experiment." *Public Opinion Quarterly*, 1994, *58*, 210–240.

Durant, L. E., Carey, M. P., and Schroder, K.E.E. "Effects of Anonymity, Gender, and Erotophilia on the Quality of Data Obtained from Self-Reports of Socially Sensitive Behaviors." *Journal of Behavioral Medicine*, 2002, *25*(5), 439–467.

Gunsalus, C. K. "Rethinking Protections for Human Subjects." *Chronicle of Higher Education*, 2002, *49*(12), B24.

Harrison, L. "The Validity of Self-Reported Drug Use in Survey Research: An Overview and Critique of Research Methods." In C. Turner, J. Lessler, and J. Gfroerer (eds.), *Survey Measurement of Drug Use: Methodological Studies.* (Department of Health and Human Services pub. no. ADM-92–1929) Rockville, Md.: National Institute on Drug Abuse, 1997.

Marquis, K. H., Marquis, M. S., and Polich, J. M. "Response Bias and Reliability in Sensitive Topic Surveys." *Journal of the American Statistical Association*, June 1986, *81*, 381–389.

National Institute of Alcohol Abuse and Alcoholism. *Certificates of Confidentiality: Protecting the Identity of Research Subjects.* Bethesda, Md.: National Institute of Alcohol Abuse and Alcoholism, 2002. [http://www.niaaa.nih.gov/extramural/confidential.htm].

National Commission for the Protection of Human Subjects of Biomedical and Behavioral Research. *The Belmont Report.* Bethesda, Md.: Office of Human Subjects Research, 1979. [http://ohsr.od.nih.gov/mpa/belmont.php3]. Access date: Jan. 21, 2004.

Pryor, J., and Keeling, R. P. *Understanding the Patterns and Priorities of Health on Campus: Net Results.* Washington, D.C.: National Association of Student Personnel Administrators, 2002. [http://www.naspa.org/netresults/article.cfm?ID=881&category=Feature]. Access date: Jan. 21, 2004.

Tourangeau, R., and Smith, T. W. "Asking Sensitive Questions: The Impact of Data Collection Mode, Question Format, and Question Context." *Public Opinion Quarterly*, 1996, *60*, 275–304.

Turner, C., Lessler, J., and Gfroerer, J. "Future Directions for Research and Practice." In C. Turner, J. Lessler, and J. Gfroerer (eds.), *Survey Measurement of Drug Use: Methodological Studies.* (DHHS pub. no. ADM-92–1929) Rockville, Md.: National Institute on Drug Abuse, 1992.

JOHN H. PRYOR is director of undergraduate evaluation and research at Dartmouth College, and research assistant professor of community and family medicine at Dartmouth Medical School.

A controlled experiment is used in a survey of high school students to investigate the effect on response rates of prizes awarded for responding to a survey.

Understanding the Effect of Prizes on Response Rates

Stephen R. Porter, Michael E. Whitcomb

As stated in Chapter One, around the world response rates to surveys have been falling. In response, researchers have developed various methods for increasing response rates. One popular method in institutional research is the use of lottery incentives. A lottery incentive is a postpaid reward offered to survey recipients for responding to the survey. Every recipient who responds is entered into a drawing (similar to a lottery) for one or more prizes. The use of lottery incentives may be increasing as researchers move from paper to electronic formats. Unlike as with mailed surveys, it is impossible to include prepaid incentives such as a dollar bill with an e-mail survey or an e-mail notice about a Web survey (Couper, 2000). Incentives paid upon completion, however, are possible with Web surveys, because these can always be mailed to respondents after the survey has been completed.

Although lottery incentives appear to be a popular and perhaps growing method for increasing response rates, the extensive survey research literature on postpaid and lottery incentives indicates that they have little or no impact on survey response (Church, 1993; James and Bolstein, 1992; Singer, van Hoewyk, and Maher, 2000; Warriner and others, 1996). When applied to higher education, however, this research may not be relevant. Previous studies have been conducted on members of the general population and it may be possible that college students are more price-sensitive than the average person. If so, lottery incentives may have an impact on rates of response to student surveys while not having any impact on rates of response to surveys of the general population.

Unfortunately, no research has been conducted on the impact of lottery incentives on student survey response rates. The lack of research in this *has this has been updated?* area seems surprising given the reliance of higher education on survey data in the decision-making processes, declining response rates, and the scarce resources of many institutions. Together these issues make student survey response rates increasingly relevant to administrators who wish to tap student feedback and opinion as part of their decision-making processes.

The reason behind the limited amount of research done on student survey response rates lies in the difficulty of testing the effectiveness of incentives in student surveys: at least two randomly selected groups of students must be used, with a control group receiving only a survey, and one or more experimental groups receiving both a survey and an incentive. Comparing response rates across different administrations of a survey (such as across years) instead of using randomized groups will not work, because other factors besides a change in survey administration may affect response rates. A similar rationale holds for comparing surveys across institutions, because school effects become confused with incentive effects.

Yet using randomized control and experimental groups within an institution poses a problem for any college or university, because students in the control group will discover that other students may win a prize for filling out the same survey. Given communication among students and the likely negative reaction of the control group, successful implementation of a controlled experiment of incentives is simply not possible on our campuses: response rates may be lower for the control group simply because members of the group react negatively to the news that they were not offered an incentive.

We circumvented this problem by conducting a controlled experiment on high school students who had contacted the admissions office at a selective liberal arts college for information about applying. Because the college draws students from across the nation, we were able to split the survey sample into groups without worrying about communication between groups. In addition, because the high school students were seniors about to attend college, their sensitivity to a lottery incentive was much more like that of the typical college student than like that of a member of the general population.

Literature Review

The empirical research on incentives indicates a conclusive positive impact on response rates; however, this impact depends very much on the type of incentive used. Incentives can be divided into two groups based on when the survey recipient receives the incentive: either with the survey (known as prepayment) or after the survey has been completed and returned (known as postpayment).

Numerous studies of various populations have examined the impact of prepaid incentives on survey response and the results indicate that their use invariably increases response rates (Church, 1993; Fox, Crask, and Kim,

1988; Furse and Stewart, 1982; Heberlein and Baumgartner, 1978; Hopkins and Gullickson, 1992; James and Bolstein, 1990; Jobber and Saunders, 1988; Singer, Groves, and Corning, 1999; Singer, van Hoewyk, and Maher, 1998, 2000; Willimack, Schuman, Pennell, and Lepkowski, 1995; Yammarino, Skinner, and Childers, 1991; Zusman and Duby, 1987). The most commonly used prepaid incentive is the inclusion of $1 or $2 with the initial mailing of the survey, with some researchers using $5 payments (for example, Singer, van Hoewyk, and Maher, 2000) or $10 payments (such as Warriner and others, 1996). Zusman and Duby (1987) found a substantial effect from a $1 prepayment to a postsecondary student sample of stopouts, finding an increase in response rate of almost 19 percentage points.

The relationship between size of incentive and survey response is less clear. Some scholars (Heberlein and Baumgartner, 1978; Hubbard and Little, 1988; James and Bolstein, 1990, 1992; Kropf, Scheib, and Blair, 1999) have found that increasing the value of a prepaid incentive leads to higher response rates, although the impact appears to taper off as the value of the incentive increases (Fox, Crask, and Kim, 1988; Warriner and others, 1996). Others (Jobber and Saunders, 1988, 1989) find that moving beyond a token amount has little or no impact on response rates.

Unlike the inclusion of prepaid incentives with surveys, promises of payment upon survey completion do not appear to affect respondent behavior. Several studies have been conducted that compare the impact of both prepayment and postpayment of incentives, with the general finding that promised payments for survey completion in the range of $5 to $20 have no statistically significant impact on response rates (Berk, Mathiowetz, Ward, and White, 1987; Berry and Kanouse, 1987; Singer, van Hoewyk, and Maher, 2000) and $50 (James and Bolstein, 1992). The same holds true for nonmonetary postpaid incentives (Jobber, Mirza, and Wee, 1991). Church (1993), in his widely cited meta-analysis of seventy-four surveys that used incentives, found that rewards contingent upon the return of the survey had no significant effect on response rates. While the studies cited here used telephone or mail surveys, a meta-analysis of sixty-eight electronic surveys found that incentives actually depressed response rates slightly (Cook, Heath, and Thompson, 2000). The authors of this analysis do not describe whether the types of incentives used by the surveys under study were prepayments or postpayments, but given the logistical difficulties of prepayments in electronic surveys (Couper, 2000), it is likely that these incentives were postpayments.

The one exception in the literature is the work of Collins, Ellickson, Hays, and McCaffrey (2000). In their study of prepayments and postpayments in the eighth wave of a decade-long longitudinal study, they found a significant positive effect for a promise of payment upon survey completion. They indicate, however, that this anomalous finding is probably the result of their sample. The respondents surveyed had participated in the study for many years and had developed a close relationship with the survey team. Thus, trust and a norm of reciprocity had already been established by the time of the study and any promises of payment would be seen as much more credible than if the respondents had been contacted for the first time.

Finally, some researchers have tested the effect of lottery postpayments, in which the incentive is contingent both upon completing the survey and on the outcome of a drawing. Similar to the literature on simple postpayments, this research has found no effect on response rates from lottery incentives (Golden, Anderson, and Sharpe, 1980; Hubbard and Little, 1988; Paolillo and Lorenzi, 1984; Warriner and others, 1996). In two studies (Hubbard and Little, 1988; Warriner and others, 1996) the prize was substantial: $200 cash.

Methodology

The experiment was conducted in spring 2001 during a survey of nonapplicant high school students (see Porter and Whitcomb, 2003, for more details). These prospective students had contacted the institution for information about the institution during the previous year but had not applied for admission.

This survey was chosen for the lottery incentives experiment for two reasons. First, by surveying high school students rather than college students, we could vary the incentive offered without worrying about contacts between members of different experimental groups. Such an experiment would be impossible to conduct on a single college campus, and using a group of colleges with varying incentives would confound school effects with incentive effects. Second, these students were expected to have little motivation to complete the survey, because they had not applied to this college. Research has shown that incentives have the largest effect when there are few reasons to participate (Singer, 2002), so using this survey should maximize the impact that lottery incentives have on response rates.

Of approximately 13,000 prospects, 9,305 had provided enough information about their high school during the contact to allow the assignment of the appropriate College Entrance Examination Board code for their high school. Because it was essential that members of the control group not discover that other students had been offered an incentive for response, students were grouped by high school for the experiment. The average number of students per high school was 2.64, with the number of students ranging from 1 to 93.

The high schools were first randomly divided into five groups: a control group and four incentive groups. By randomly selecting high schools rather than students, we ensured that students in the same high school were placed into the same experimental group and therefore would not discover via communication with friends that others in their high school had received a different incentive offer.

The survey instrument was adapted from the College Board's Admitted Student Questionnaire and comprised six topics: importance of college characteristics, characteristic ratings for the university, role of financial aid in the application process, images of the university, number of applications mailed, and demographic information. The survey administration consisted of an initial e-mail notification with an embedded survey link, and each group was administered the same survey. Although students were asked to enter their e-mail address during the survey, the sample groups were given links to five separate Web sites to ensure that we could track differences between groups. The four incentive groups were informed that if they responded to the survey they would be entered into a drawing for either a $50, $100, $150, or $200 gift certificate, depending on the experimental condition, to the online retailer Amazon.com. The e-mails sent to each group were identical except for the e-mails sent to the incentive groups, which included this additional passage about the lottery incentive: "Because we realize your time is valuable, when you complete the survey you will be entered into a drawing for a $_____ gift certificate from Amazon.com. The drawing will be held within six weeks and you will be notified of the outcome via e-mail." In accordance with Schaefer and Dillman (1998), the initial e-mail was followed three days later by a reminder e-mail to nonrespondents, and by a final reminder to nonrespondents five days after the first reminder. Each reminder included details about the particular incentive for each group.

Results

In all analyses, we examined the control and experimental groups to investigate three main questions:

- Do all five groups (the control and four levels of incentive) differ from one another?
- Does each incentive level differ individually from the control group?
- Do respondents offered any sort of incentive differ from those not offered an incentive?

The first question tests whether increasing levels of incentives have a differential impact; in other words, do response rates increase as the amount of the incentive increases? This is a common view of incentives and their impact on response rates: more is better (Heberlein and Baumgartner, 1978; Hubbard and Little, 1988; James and Bolstein, 1990, 1992; Kropf, Scheib, and Blair, 1999).

The second question tests if only some of the incentives have an impact. For example, there may be a nonlinear relationship between response rates and incentive amounts, as some researchers have found when looking at prepaid incentives (Fox, Crask, and Kim, 1988; Warriner and others,

1996). Small amounts may have little impact because the respondent does not feel they are adequate to justify his or her expenditure of time. Large amounts, on the other hand, may have little impact because respondents are skeptical that they will receive the prize given its large value. Alternatively, large amounts may be viewed as compensation rather than as a token benefit, thus transforming the relationship from one of reciprocity to an economic one. As a result, small amounts would invoke a norm of reciprocity and increase the probability of responding, while large amounts would invoke an economic relationship and not affect the probability of responding.

The third question tests the overall impact of offering an incentive. Some research has indicated that there may not be much of a difference in response rates between the $50 group and the $200 group (Jobber and Saunders, 1988, 1989), and depending on the data, ANOVA testing for differences between all five groups could result in a null finding. Yet ANOVA testing the control versus all the incentive groups might detect a positive impact, so this third hypothesis is simply another way to check the data.

Table 4.1 shows the response rates for the initial e-mail and the response rates at the close of the experiment. Rates are shown for each of the five groups, for the four incentive groups combined, and for the entire sample. Overall 15.2 percent of the sample responded to the survey. Differences between the control group and the incentive groups were quite small. Almost 14 percent of the control group responded, while overall 15.6 percent of respondents in the incentive groups participated in the survey.

A series of chi-square tests were conducted to test for differences in response rates. Given previous research indicating that the impact of incentives may vary with the number of contacts (James and Bolstein, 1990), we examined response rates both following the initial e-mail requesting survey participation and at the end of survey administration. As seen in Table 4.2, only one significant finding emerged: at the conclusion of the survey the response rate for those offered the $100 incentive (16.2 percent) was significantly greater than the response rate for the control group (13.9 percent), χ^2 (1) = 3.93, p = 0.047. This finding may imply that the relationship between incentive amount and survey response is nonlinear; however, given our large sample size combined with the marginal p-value, as well as the weak substantive impact of a 2.3 percent increase in response rate, the support these data give for a nonlinear effect is limited.

In addition to examining the effect of incentives on response rates, we also tested whether our experimental conditions had any effect on the quality of survey responses. It is possible that an incentive might not change the probability that an individual will respond to a survey, but it might cause respondents to spend more time answering the survey questions (James and Bolstein, 1990; Singer, van Hoewyk, and Maher, 1998, 2000; Willimack, Schuman, Pennell, and Lepkowski, 1995). One way to test this hypothesis is to test item nonresponse between the experimental groups. If this

Table 4.1. Initial and Final Response Rates by Incentive Group

Group	After 1st e-mail	After 3rd e-mail
Control (no incentive)	4.6%	13.9%
Incentive $50	5.4%	15.0%
Incentive $100	5.3%	16.2%
Incentive $150	6.0%	15.6%
Incentive $200	5.8%	15.4%
All incentive groups	5.6%	15.6%
Total sample	5.4%	15.2%

Table 4.2. Hypotheses and Tests for Differences in Response Rates

	Dependent Variable: Response Rate					
	After 1st e-mail			After 3rd e-mail		
Hypothesis	χ^2	df	p<	χ^2	df	p<
Control ≠ $50 ≠ $100 ≠ $150 ≠ $200	4.27	4	.371	4.30	4	.367
Control ≠ $50	1.26	1	.262	0.97	1	.324
Control ≠ $100	1.03	1	.310	3.93	1	.047
Control ≠ $150	3.45	1	.063	2.15	1	.142
Control ≠ $200	2.97	1	.085	1.74	1	.187
Control ≠ all incentive groups combined	3.17	1	.075	3.36	1	.067

hypothesis were true, we would expect lower item nonresponse for respondents in the incentive groups, because respondents who wished to breeze through the survey would be more likely to leave questions unanswered.

For each respondent, we calculated separately the number of survey items completed in each of the first five sections; these scores served as dependent measures in a series of one-way ANOVAs. For the demographic variables, we recorded whether or not respondents supplied the requested information, and we used the resultant binary data (0 = did not supply; 1 = supplied) in a series of chi-square tests.

In the series of one-way ANOVAs, we examined whether (1) the number of survey items were completed, or (2) the mean responses given varied across the survey conditions. As in the earlier analyses, we tested the three main research questions outlined earlier. We found no significant findings for the number of items completed for the importance of characteristics, financial aid, or images of the institution, or for the provision of demographic information. Significant effects of lottery incentives were found only for the importance of college characteristics and the number of college applications. Respondents in the $50, $100, and $200 incentive groups completed more items than respondents in the control group, with means of 16.8, 16.8, 16.9, and 16.3 (out of seventeen items), respectively.

Additionally, a significant effect of the overall impact of offering incentives was found for the number of characteristics ratings completed, with respondents offered incentives completing significantly more items (mean = 16.75) than the control (mean = 16.29). These findings suggest that the use of incentives may have caused respondents to complete a greater number of items specific to the university offering the reward, while more general survey questions were completed at a rate that was identical to that of respondents not offered an incentive. The substantive difference is quite small, however: about 0.5 items.

Analysis of the number of college applications found that respondents in the $200 incentive group applied to significantly more schools (mean = 5.6) than the control group did (mean = 5.0). This finding can be interpreted two ways. The first interpretation posits that the possibility of a large reward caused respondents in the largest incentive category to complete the survey more thoroughly than the other respondents did. The second and more plausible interpretation is that this finding is simply spurious. Using the .05 error level in multiple tests, we would expect to have significant results when there is actually no relationship (Type I error) in five out of one hundred tests. If the first interpretation were true, we would have expected the analyses to reveal a larger number of significant findings.

To compare opinions of the survey groups on the importance of college characteristics in the application process and in the characteristic rating section of the survey, we conducted a series of one-way ANOVAs using the mean response to each item as the dependent measure. Of the 204 tests conducted (34 survey items times 6 comparisons), only 6 (2.9 percent) were found to be significant. Because the number of significant effects was about what we might expect to find erroneously (at $p < .05$), we concluded that these (significant) findings were spurious.

In sum, the offer of a $100 gift certificate in a drawing increased the response rate by 2 percentage points, but there were no other significant differences between the control and incentive groups. Given the very large sample size and p value (only .047), this is a weak finding, especially in terms of the substantive effect. In addition, it does not appear that offering larger amounts of incentives has a positive impact on response. There was some evidence that members of the incentive groups spent more time on the survey, as indicated by a slightly smaller item nonresponse rate. Again, the substantive differences were small.

Discussion

Although the literature on incentives and response rates shows that postpayment of incentives in general and lotteries in particular has little or no impact on survey response, use of such lottery incentives appears common in institutional research. Our research is in line with previous research on the general population that shows the minimal effect of postpaid incentives. Using a control group and four experimental groups, we tested the impact of offering a prize for survey participation in a national Web survey in which respondents had little reason to participate. By using high school students from around the country, we were able to test the impact of incentives on a population very similar to the typical college student population. Also, by using a survey in which respondents had little reason to participate, we had a situation where incentives should have had a large effect.

Although the prizes ranged in size from $50 to $200, the response rates for the five groups were very similar, ranging from 13.9 percent to 16.2 percent. Two of these response rates differed significantly: students in the group that was promised to be entered into a drawing for a $100 gift certificate had a response rate 2.3 percentage points higher than the control group. Although this difference was significant, in terms of substantive results the offer of a $100 gift certificate had a minimal impact.

Assuming that this result is not a spurious finding, it raises the question of how researchers should select the prizes to be offered for survey participation. Our results indicate that more is *not* better: increasing the size of the prize did not result in a linear increase in response rates. Researchers are thus faced with a quandary. If the prize is not valuable enough, it will not affect response rates. If the prize is too valuable, it also will not affect response rates. It is likely, then, that resources might be spent on prizes that in turn will not affect the survey response rate.

In addition, our research raises the serious question of effectiveness and resource allocation. Given limited resources, should we be spending time and money on awarding prizes, or on efforts that have proved to increase response rates, such as Dillman's (2000) method of personalized, multiple contacts? It is tempting to offer large prizes in a survey, because to individuals unfamiliar with survey research methodology, it appears as if strong efforts have been made to increase response rates. A few large prizes may also be cheaper than including $1 or $2 prepayments with all surveys. Less striking efforts such as a second or third mailing or a personalized letter salutation may be less appealing but offer more certain benefits.

Lottery incentives may also be popular because the inclusion of money with a survey may appear unseemly or cause resentment among college students, most of whom are paying (or whose parents are paying) substantial amounts of money to attend college. Offering a prize circumvents these concerns. Given the null findings of this study as well as previous research concerning the effect of prizes on survey response, one approach that researchers may adopt in the future is the inclusion of a promise of a small charitable contribution with a survey. Several scholars, however, have studied how offers of contributions to charity affect response rates and have concluded that promised charitable contributions have no effect on respondent behavior (Furse and Stewart, 1982; Hubbard and Little, 1988; Warriner and others, 1996).

A final concern is the extent to which paying students to participate in survey research may create expectation effects that will negatively affect future surveys. The current research indicates that this is a nonissue (Singer, van Hoewyk, and Maher, 1998, 2000; Singer, Groves, and Corning, 1999). These studies, however, tested the impact of incentives on subsequent survey response after a six-month or twelve-month period. It is less clear if using incentives in multiple surveys of the same population over several years, which is rapidly becoming the norm at many institutions, would also have a minimal impact on survey response rates.

As response rates to student surveys continue to decline, educational researchers will increasingly have to weight survey responses using administrative data about respondents and nonrespondents (see, for example, Dey, 1997; Zanutto and Zaslavsky, 2002). Yet statistical adjustments of our survey data cannot completely correct for a low response rate: we must also focus more of our efforts on collecting reliable data. Only by using methods confirmed by experimental testing can we understand what works and be assured of maximizing the return on our survey research expenditures.

[handwritten margin note: e.g. focus groups?]

References

Berk, M. L., Mathiowetz, N. A., Ward, E. P., and White, A. A. "The Effect of Prepaid and Promised Incentives: Results of a Controlled Experiment." *Journal of Official Statistics,* 1987, *3*(4), 449–457.

Berry, S. H., and Kanouse, D. E. "Physician Response to a Mailed Survey: An Experiment in Timing of Payment. *Public Opinion Quarterly,* 1987, *51,* 102–114.

Church, A. "Estimating the Effect of Incentives on Mail Survey Response Rates: A Meta-analysis." *Public Opinion Quarterly,* 1993, *57,* 62–79.

Collins, R. L., Ellickson, P. L., Hays, R. D., and McCaffrey, D. F. "Effects of Incentive Size and Timing on Response Rates to a Follow-up of a Longitudinal Mailed Survey." *Evaluation Review,* 2000, *24*(4), 347–363.

Cook, C., Heath, F., and Thompson, R. L. "A Meta-analysis of Response Rates in Web- or Internet-Based Surveys. *Educational and Psychological Measurement,* 2000, *60*(6), 821–836.

Couper, M. "Web Surveys: A Review of Issues and Approaches. *Public Opinion Quarterly,* 2000, *64,* 464–494.

Dey, E. "Working with Low Survey Response Rates: The Efficacy of Weighting Adjustments." *Research in Higher Education,* 1997, *38*(2), 215–227.

Dillman, D. A. *Mail and Internet Surveys: The Tailored Design Method.* New York: Wiley, 2000.

Fox, R. J., Crask, M. R., and Kim, J. "Mail Survey Response Rate: A Meta-analysis of Selected Techniques for Inducing Response." *Public Opinion Quarterly,* 1988, *52,* 467–491.

Furse, D. H., and Stewart, D. W. "Monetary Incentives Versus Promised Contribution to Charity: New Evidence on Mail Survey Response." *Journal of Market Research,* 1982, *19,* 375–380.

Golden, L.L., Anderson, W. T., and Sharpe, L. K. "The Effects of Salutation, Monetary Incentive, and Degree of Urbanization on Mail Questionnaire Response Rate, Speed and Quality." In Monroe, K. B. (ed.), *Advances in Consumer Research.* Ann Arbor, Mich.: Association for Consumer Research, 1980.

Heberlein, T. A., and Baumgartner, R. "Factors Affecting Response Rates to Mailed

Questionnaires: A Quantitative Analysis of the Published Literature." *American Sociological Review*, 1978, *43*(4), 447–462.

Hopkins, K. D., and Gullickson, A. R. "Response Rates in Survey Research: A Meta-analysis of the Effects of Monetary Gratuities." *Journal of Experimental Education*, 1992, *61*(1), 52–62.

Hubbard, R., and Little, E. L. "Promised Contributions to Charity and Mail Survey Responses: Replication with Extension." *Public Opinion Quarterly*, 1988, *52*, 223–230.

James, J., and Bolstein, R. "The Effect of Monetary Incentives and Follow-up Mailings on the Response Rate and Response Quality in Mail Surveys." *Public Opinion Quarterly*, 1990, *54*, 346–361.

James, J., and Bolstein, R. "Large Monetary Incentives and Their Effect on Mail Survey Response Rates." *Public Opinion Quarterly*, 1992, *56*, 442–453.

Jobber, D., Mirza, H., and Wee, K. H. "Incentives and Response Rates to Cross-National Business Surveys: A Logit Model Analysis." *Journal of International Business Studies*, 1991, *22*(4), 711–721.

Jobber, D., and Saunders, J. "Modeling the Effects of Prepaid Monetary Incentives on Mail Survey Response." *Journal of the Operational Research Society*, 1988, *39*(4), 365–372.

Jobber, D., and Saunders, J. "The Prediction of Industrial Mail-Survey Response Rates." *Journal of the Operational Research Society*, 1989, *40*(10), 839–847.

Kropf, M. E., Scheib, J., and Blair, J. *The Effect of Alternative Incentives on Cooperation and Refusal Conversion in a Telephone Survey.* College Park: University of Maryland, Survey Research Center, 1999.

Paolillo, J., and Lorenzi, P. "Monetary Incentives and Mail Questionnaire Response Rates." *Journal of Advertising*, 1984, *13*, 46–48.

Porter, S. R., and Whitcomb, M. W. "The Impact of Lottery Incentives on Student Survey Response Rates." *Research in Higher Education*, 2003, *44*(4), 389–407.

Schaefer, D. R., and Dillman, D. A. "Development of a Standard E-mail Methodology: Results of an Experiment." *Public Opinion Quarterly*, 1998, *62*, 378–397.

Singer, E. "The Use of Incentives to Reduce Nonresponse in Household Surveys." In R. M. Groves, D. A. Dillman, J. L. Eltinge, and R.J.A. Little, (eds.), *Survey Nonresponse.* New York: Wiley, 2002.

Singer, E., Groves, R. M., and Corning, A. D. "Differential Incentives: Beliefs About Practices, Perceptions of Equity, and Effects on Survey Participation." *Public Opinion Quarterly*, 1999, *63*, 251–260.

Singer, E., van Hoewyk, J., and Maher, M. P. "Does the Payment of Incentives Create Expectation Effects?" *Public Opinion Quarterly*, 1998, *62*, 152–164.

Singer, E., van Hoewyk, J., and Maher, M. "Experiments with Incentives in Telephone Surveys." *Public Opinion Quarterly*, 2000, *64*, 171–188.

Smith, T. "Trends in Nonresponse Rates." *International Journal of Public Opinion Research*, 1995, *7*, 157–171.

Warriner, K., and others. "Charities, No; Lotteries, No; Cash, Yes: Main Effects and Interactions in a Canadian Incentives Experiment." *Public Opinion Quarterly*, 1996, *60*, 542–562.

Willimack, D., Schuman, H., Pennell, B., and Lepkowski, J. "Effects of a Prepaid Nonmonetary Incentive on Response Rates and Response Quality in a Face-to-Face Survey. *Public Opinion Quarterly*, 1995, *59*, 78–92.

Yammarino, F. J., Skinner, S. J., and Childers, T. L. "Understanding Mail Survey Response Behavior: A Meta-analysis." *Public Opinion Quarterly*, 1991, *55*, 613–639.

Zanutto, E., and Zaslavsky, A. "Using Administrative Records to Impute for Nonresponse." In R. M. Groves, D. A. Dillman, J. L. Eltinge, and R.J.A. Little (eds.), *Survey Nonresponse.* New York: Wiley, 2002.

Zusman, B. J., and Duby, P. "An Evaluation of the Use of Monetary Incentives in Postsecondary Survey Research." *Journal of Research and Development in Education,* 1987, *20*(4), 73–78.

STEPHEN R. PORTER *is director of institutional research at Wesleyan University.*

MICHAEL E. WHITCOMB *is assistant director of institutional research at Wesleyan University.*

This chapter reviews the literature on survey fatigue and summarizes a research project that indicates that administering multiple surveys in one academic year can significantly suppress response rates in later surveys.

Multiple Surveys of Students and Survey Fatigue

Stephen R. Porter, Michael E. Whitcomb,
William H. Weitzer

As described in Chapter One, survey nonresponse has been increasing both in the United States and internationally, and much of this nonresponse is due to rising rates of refusal. In many discussions about the rise in survey nonresponse, survey fatigue is often cited as one possible cause. Steeh (1981, p. 53), for example, cites "overexposure to the survey process," while de Heer (1999) notes some interesting variations in the number of surveys being conducted in different countries as influencing response rates across countries.

Despite the view that rising nonresponse rates are in part caused by an increase in the number of surveys, there has been almost no research on the impact of multiple survey requests on survey response. In part this is not surprising, because most research on survey nonresponse analyzes only one survey and thus focuses on a single point in time (Harris-Kojetin and Tucker, 1999). Yet the issue of survey fatigue will become increasingly important as the costs of designing and administering a survey decrease. A variety of software products now allow anyone with minimal technical skills to create and administer a simple Web survey.

This issue is also of vital importance to research in higher education, as the use of student surveys in assessment and institutional research continues to increase. A large array of national surveys that together can be used to describe and assess almost any facet of the undergraduate experience are currently available. Most colleges and universities have their own internally designed surveys as well. Add to the mix the growing pressures for assessment from outside groups such as legislatures and accrediting agencies, and internal pressures from individual offices trying to show performance results and the pressure to administer multiple surveys can be intense.

Even if the number of surveys on a campus is limited, the timing of the surveys could be such that two surveys may overlap or be administered back-to-back. On many campuses this may even happen unknowingly, as different offices administer their particular survey unaware of the actions of other offices. Educational researchers must understand the impact of multiple surveys on response rates in order to appropriately design and implement their surveys. Understanding the impact of multiple surveys can allow an institution to juggle various demands and can also act as an impetus for the development of a survey research policy.

Quantifying the impact of survey fatigue is also useful for individual institutions grappling with demands for surveys from numerous internal constituencies. For larger schools, multiple surveys do not necessarily pose a problem, because many large samples of students can be drawn without surveying the same students twice. For smaller schools, however, conducting multiple surveys inevitably means that the same students will be surveyed multiple times.

This chapter describes two experiments conducted at a selective liberal arts college to quantify the impact of multiple survey requests on student survey response behavior. We seek to answer two questions. First, does implementing multiple student surveys have a negative effect on later surveys? Second, if so, does this effect vary by subpopulations of students?

Previous Research

Survey fatigue is one component of respondent burden, generally defined as the time and effort involved in participating in a survey (Sharp and Frankel, 1983). Much of the research on respondent burden has focused on interview length and has generally found that longer surveys result in lower response rates (see the discussion in Chapter One of this volume). Although little research has been done on the impact of multiple surveys on response rates, research on respondent burden sheds some light on the potential impact of survey fatigue. This research can be divided into three areas. The first looks at nonresponse in panel surveys, in which respondents are interviewed several times during a research project rather than just once. The second area of research uses surveys to query nonrespondents about reasons for their behavior. The third area actually analyzes the impact of multiple (different) survey requests on survey nonresponse, the topic of this chapter.

Panel Surveys. Some scholars have looked at respondent burden in panel surveys. Because panel surveys involve several survey iterations, refusals to participate are expected to rise over time because of the increasing burden on the respondent. Thus, increasing nonresponse is a common feature in panel surveys (Kalton, Kasprzyk, and McMillen, 1989). For example, using several federal government household panel surveys, Atrostic, Bates, Burt, and Silberstein (2001) found refusal rates to increase with each subsequent interview, although this pattern began to taper off after the first few interviews.

Interestingly, one study compared response rates in an experiment that altered the protocol used when approaching members of the sample for a panel survey (Apodaca, Lea, and Edwards, 1998). Simply informing respondents that if they chose to participate in the current interview they would be contacted again several times over the next few years for additional interviews reduced response rates by 5 percentage points. These results, along with the general research on refusal rates in panel surveys, indicate that not only do respondents initially balk at participating in a survey with several interview components, but also some of those who initially agree refuse to participate in later interviews. Clearly multiple surveys are perceived as a burden by respondents, and we would expect response rates to decrease as the number of survey requests increases.

Surveys About Surveys. Research on survey behavior is another area that sheds some light on survey fatigue. In a telephone follow-up of nonrespondents to a mail survey, researchers queried for the most important reason why they had not responded to the survey (Sosdian and Sharp, 1980). Twenty percent said they "never got around to it," implying a possible lack of time to participate, while 17 percent replied "too busy," and 7 percent said that the survey came "at a bad time" in their personal schedule. Only 1 percent said that the survey was too long. Taken together, these comments indicate that time is an issue in survey response, with the implication that the more time is demanded, as in multiple surveys, the lower the response rate will be.

From a higher education perspective, a research project conducted by the U.S. Air Force Academy (Asiu, Antons, and Fultz, 1998) provides important information. Faced with anecdotal evidence that students were frustrated by the number of surveys being conducted, researchers used focus groups and a survey to determine students' attitudes toward surveys at the Academy. The results are striking. Almost all of the respondents (97 percent) stated that they felt "somewhat" oversurveyed, with almost half (48 percent) stating that "yes, definitely" they felt oversurveyed. When asked, the students indicated that they should be surveyed only three or four times a year.

Interestingly, a content analysis of student definitions of the term *oversurveyed* revealed that students felt oversurveyed because of "the combination of frequent surveys that are perceived as irrelevant to daily student (cadet) life." This result indicates that survey fatigue may depend on salience, and that the impact of multiple survey administrations may vary not just because of the number of surveys but because of their content as well.

Studies of Survey Fatigue. Our literature review revealed two studies of the impact of survey fatigue on nonpanel surveys, that is, multiple surveys from different projects conducted over time. Each study reached a different conclusion about the effect of survey fatigue on response rates. The first study looked at a series of farm surveys conducted over time by the U.S. Department of Agriculture (McCarthy and Beckler, 1999). This study found no relationship between the number of times participants were previously contacted by the USDA and the response rates in a later survey. The second study asked respondents the number of times they had been previously contacted to participate in a survey and found a strong negative relationship between the number of previous survey contacts and participation in a later survey (Goyder, 1986).

From all of these studies we can conclude the following:

- The prospect of multiple surveys can reduce response rates.
- Nonrespondents often cite time concerns as reasons for nonresponse, implying that as the amount of time spent participating in surveys increases, survey nonresponse will increase.
- The effects of survey fatigue may be moderated by the salience of survey content.
- The number of previous surveys may have an impact on current survey response, although the evidence here is mixed.

Two Tests of Survey Fatigue

Using several undergraduate student surveys, we conducted two experiments at a selective liberal arts college to measure the impact of survey fatigue and whether it may have a greater impact on some subpopulations than on others. The first study looks at the impact of a paper survey administered immediately prior to a second paper survey. The second looks at the impact of three Web surveys administered during the fall semester on a Web survey administered during the following spring semester.

Experiment I. The first experiment took place in spring 2001 and used two surveys administered to the senior class ($n = 649$). The class was randomly divided into two groups, with the first group receiving two surveys and the second group receiving one survey. The first group was administered the College Student Experiences Questionnaire (CSEQ) during the last week of March and the first three weeks of April. This paper questionnaire is seven pages long and was administered with a prenotification e-mail, a first mailing of the survey via campus mail, an e-mail reminder to all members of the sample, a second mailing of the survey via campus mail to nonrespondents, and an e-mail reminder to nonrespondents. The response rate was 28 percent.

Beginning in the last week of April and extending into May, all seniors were administered the Senior Survey, an eight-page paper questionnaire asking questions about future plans and about satisfaction with various aspects of their undergraduate education. Survey administration consisted of a

Table 5.1. Experiment I: Senior Survey Response Rates

	Senior Survey response rate (%)		Differences in response rates between groups (percentage points)	Sample sizes	
	No prior surveys (A)	1 prior survey (B)	(B-A)	(A)	(B)
All students	67	57	−10**	324	325
Gender					
Female	70	59	−11*	173	174
Male	64	54	−10†	151	151
Difference			−1		
Race					
White	72	59	−13**	197	220
Nonwhite	60	52	−7	127	105
Difference			−5		
1st semester GPA					
A	71	59	−12*	159	172
B or less	63	54	−9	165	153
Difference			−4		

*Response rates differ significantly at the $p < .05$ level.

** Response rates differ significantly at the $p < .01$ level.

†Response rates differ significantly at the $p < .10$ level.

paper prenotification letter, a first mailing of the survey via campus mail, an e-mail reminder to nonrespondents, a second mailing of the survey via campus mail to nonrespondents, and a second e-mail reminder to nonrespondents. Additionally, an in-person request for survey completion was asked of all nonrespondents when they went to pick up their diploma at the end of the survey administration period. The overall response rate was 62 percent.

Both surveys used Dillman's (2000) method of survey administration, which emphasizes several contacts with respondents, and the two surveys were conducted almost back-to-back. Table 5.1 illustrates the impact of the first survey administration: students who were mailed the CSEQ prior to the administration of the Senior Survey had a Senior Survey response rate 10 percentage points lower than seniors who were not asked to participate in the CSEQ (57 percent and 67 percent, respectively).

Looking at response rates by gender, race, and grade-point average (GPA), there are some interesting differences for some subgroups. Survey fatigue appeared to affect females and males equally. For whites alone, the prior survey had a statistically significant impact on response rates (−13 percentage points), but the difference for nonwhites (−7 percentage points) was not statistically significant. A better test of differential impact is whether these two differences differ from one another. This difference, -5 percentage points, is not statistically significant. The same relationship holds for the two GPA groups. While the results hint at a larger impact for whites and A students, we cannot conclude that this is indeed the case. The lack of statistical significance is likely due to the small number of participants in our study.

Experiment II. The second experiment took place during the 2002–2003 academic year and used four Web surveys administered throughout the academic year to the class of first-year students. The first-year students were randomly selected into four groups. The first group (A) was asked to take only one survey during the entire academic year, a consortium survey about academic experiences called the Enrolled Student Survey. The second group (B) was asked to take two surveys, an internal survey about campus dining services and the Enrolled Student Survey. The third group (C) was administered the dining and Enrolled Student Surveys as well as a national drug survey called the Core Alcohol and Drug Survey. Finally, the fourth group (D) was administered four different surveys: an internal survey evaluating our new student orientation program, the Core survey, the dining survey, and the Enrolled Student Survey. Table 5.2 shows the experimental design and sample sizes for each group. The orientation survey was conducted in the last two weeks of October, the Core survey in the first two weeks of November, the Dining Services Survey in the last two weeks of November, and the Enrolled Student Survey in March.

The surveys were conducted in a similar manner, with students notified via an e-mail that contained a hyperlink to the survey Web site. The first, third, and fourth surveys consisted of an initial e-mail and two reminder e-mails to nonrespondents. The Core survey was conducted anonymously, with an initial e-mail and only one reminder to all members of the sample.

Table 5.2 presents the response rates for the orientation, Core, dining, and Enrolled Student Surveys. It is fairly clear that the response rate drops for an experimental group if there was a previous survey. Group A took only one survey and had a response rate of 60 percent. Group B took two surveys and the response rate dropped from 68 percent to 63 percent. Group C took three surveys and the response rate fluctuated from 54 percent to 58 percent to 47 percent. Group D dropped from 70 percent to 44 percent to 46 percent to 47 percent. One inconsistent data point for Group C is the dining survey response rates. Here the response rate is higher for the second survey, most likely due to the high salience of the dining survey among students. Also note that the decline tends to level off at the mid-40 percent range for Group D. It is reasonable to speculate that there are "hard-core" survey responders who will not be fatigued by multiple surveys, hence the impact of survey fatigue may not be strictly linear.

By looking at the first diagonal in Table 5.2, which contains the response rates for the first survey administered to each experimental group,

Table 5.2. Experiment II: First Year Student's Response Rates

		Response rate (%)			
Group	Sample size	Orientation (late Oct.)	Core (early Nov.)	Dining Services (late Nov.)	Enrolled Student (March)
A	144	—	—	—	60
B	144	—	—	68	63
C	144	—	54	58	47
D	144	70	44	46	47
Total	576	70	49	52	54

it is possible to see the effect of each survey's salience and timing on survey response. If survey attributes did not influence survey participation, the response rates across this diagonal would not vary, but they do. Looking at the first survey response rate for Groups A through D, the results are varied: 70 percent (orientation), 54 percent (Core Survey), 68 percent (Dining Services), and 60 percent (Enrolled Student). However, by looking at the timing and salience of the specific surveys, a pattern does emerge.

Although the expectation might have been that the administration of the first survey to each group would produce equivalent responses rates, it is understandable that new students might be more inclined to fill out a specific survey about their orientation experience than the other students were to fill out the first survey they received. Similarly, it is not surprising that first-semester students would answer a short, specific, and salient survey about dining services at a greater rate than second-semester students responded to a long, varied survey in March (the Enrolled Student Survey). Thus we see strong evidence that factors such as survey content and timing of administration can affect rates of participation.

Finally, regardless of the number of previous surveys, no survey achieved a response rate below 44 percent. This finding likely indicates that while survey fatigue has an impact on response rates, there may be a hardcore group of responders who will reliably complete our surveys.

Table 5.3 provides more detail about the impact of one and two previous surveys on the Dining Services Survey response rate. The first row of this table illustrates the most linear survey fatigue finding, with response rates decreasing as the number of prior surveys increases from zero to one to two (68 percent, 58 percent, and 46 percent, respectively). Here receiving invitations to participate in two previous surveys lowered response rates in the dining survey by 22 percentage points. The immediately prior survey was the Core Survey, which was long and personally intrusive. Another factor leading to the consistent results is that all three surveys were administered during one semester.

Most of the subgroups (gender, race, and GPA) follow the overall trend and show statistically significant declines in response rates. As in the first

Table 5.3. Experiment III: Dining Services Survey Response Rates

	Dining Services Survey response rates (%)			Impact on Dining Services Survey response rate (%)			Sample sizes		
	No prior surveys (Group B)	1 prior survey (Group C)	2 prior surveys (Group D)	(C-B)	(D-A)	Total impact (D-B)	(B)	(C)	(D)
All students	68	58	46	−10†	−12*	−22**	144	144	144
Gender									
Female	69	58	49	−11	−9	−20*	70	77	72
Male	68	57	43	−11	−14	−25**	74	67	72
Difference				0	5	5			
Race									
White	69	57	52	−12†	−5	−17*	91	88	95
Nonwhite	66	59	35	−7	−24*	−31**	53	56	49
Difference				−5	19	14			
1st semester GPA									
A	74	60	57	−14†	−3	−17	61	67	49
B or less	64	56	40	−8	−16*	−24**	83	77	95
Difference				−6	13	7			

*Response rates differ significantly at the $p < .05$ level.

**Response rates differ significantly at the $p < .01$ level.

†Response rates differ significantly at the $p < .10$ level.

experiment, there are no significant differences in declines between subgroups. Again, it is likely that the small number of participants had an impact when the findings were in the predicted direction but not significant.

Table 5.4 provides additional details about the impact of one, two, and three previous surveys on the Enrolled Student Survey response rate. This, the most complicated table, provides the most nuanced view of survey fatigue. The column measuring total impact (D−A) is consistently in the predicted direction and statistically significant. Here we see a significant decline, but less than in the previous table. Two things are worth noting in the first row of the table. First, the decline is not as large as in the previous table. This may be due to the administration of this survey in the spring, while all previous surveys were administered in the fall. It could be that as time passes, the impact of previous survey administrations tends to wear off. Second, the decline appears to level off after the second survey. It may be that there is a hard-core group of survey "cooperators" who are relatively unaffected by multiple survey administrations.

The column measuring the impact of the Dining Services Survey (B−A), however, is not significant overall and significant only for one subgroup (males). This may be attributed to the short, specific, and salient nature of

Table 5.4. Experiment II: Enrolled Student Survey Response Rates

	Enrolled Student Survey response rates by group (%)				Differences in response rates between groups (percentage points)				Sample sizes			
	No prior surveys (A)	1 prior survey (B)	2 prior surveys (C)	3 prior surveys (D)	(B-A)	(C-B)	(D-C)	Total impact (D-A)	(A)	(B)	(C)	(D)
All students	60	63	47	47	3	−16**	0	−13*	144	144	144	144
Gender												
Female	71	63	55	53	−8	−8	−2	−18*	77	70	77	72
Male	46	62	39	42	16†	−23**	3	−4	67	74	67	72
Difference					−24*	15	−5	−14				
Race												
White	60	66	50	55	6	−16*	5	−5	89	91	88	95
Nonwhite	60	57	43	33	−3	−14	−10	−27**	55	53	56	49
Difference					10	−2	15	22†				
1st semester GPA												
A	66	74	51	59	8	−23**	8	−7	59	61	67	49
B or less	55	54	44	41	−1	−10	−3	−14†	85	83	77	95
Difference					9	−13	12	7				

*Response rates differ significantly at the $p < .05$ level.
**Response rates differ significantly at the $p < .01$ level.
†Response rates differ significantly at the $p < .10$ level.

the Dining Services Survey. There is also no effect when looking at the impact of the orientation survey (D–C), which may possibly be attributed to the specific and salient nature of that survey. Finally, the greatest contribution to the overall difference comes from the Core Survey (C–B), which as stated above is long, although specific, but intrusive in nature.

Most of the subgroups (gender, race, and GPA) follow the overall trend and show statistically significant declines in response rates. Looking at differences between groups, there is some evidence that survey fatigue may have a differential impact among students. We can see that survey fatigue affected nonwhites more than whites, but only at an alpha level of .10. Again, it is likely that the small number of participants had an impact where the findings were in the predicted direction but not significant.

Conclusion

Although the demand for student surveys is growing, little research examines the impact of survey fatigue on response rates. Will administering multiple surveys to students eventually result in less cooperation? On the basis of the research presented here we would answer with a qualified yes. Multiple surveys do appear to suppress response rates. Yet the impact of multiple surveys is not linear. Our results indicate that survey fatigue may have the biggest impact on surveys conducted back-to-back. Surveys conducted in a previous semester may not affect response rates, or the impact may be minimal. Similarly, the impact may not be strictly linear and instead may level off over time.

Some of the results given here are obscured by salience effects as well as by timing effects. Clearly some surveys interest students more than others, and it may be that these surveys do not cause as much survey fatigue as less relevant surveys do. More research in this area is needed.

Experienced panel researchers write, "After cooperating for what can be some years of a panel, respondents may become bored or uninterested in taking part any further or *simply feel that they have 'done enough'*" (Laurie, Smith, and Scott, 1999, p. 270, emphasis added). In e-mails we have received from students who were targeted for multiple survey administrations, this feeling appears to be quiet common. Institutional researchers must be careful not to evoke such a feeling among students; otherwise, survey fatigue may become more of a problem and negatively affect future research efforts.

References

Apodaca, R., Lea, S., and Edwards, B. "The Effect of Longitudinal Burden on Survey Participation." Paper presented at the annual conference of the American Association for Public Opinion Research, St. Louis, Mo., May 1998.

Asiu, B. W., Antons, C. M., and Fultz, M. L. "Undergraduate Perceptions of Survey Participation: Improving Response Rates and Validity." Paper presented at the annual meeting of the Association of Institutional Research, Minneapolis, Minn., May 1998.

Atrostic, B. K., Bates, N., Burt, G., and Silberstein, A. "Nonresponse in U.S. Government Household Surveys: Consistent Measures, Recent Trends, and New Insights." *Journal of Official Statistics*, 2001, *17*(2), 209–226.

de Heer, W. "International Response Trends: Results of an International Survey." *Journal of Official Statistics*, 1999, *15*(2), 129–142.

Dillman, D. A. *Mail and Internet Surveys: The Tailored Design Method.* New York: Wiley, 2000.

Goyder, J. "Surveys on Surveys: Limitations and Potentialities." *Public Opinion Quarterly*, 1986, *50*(1), 27–41.

Harris-Kojetin, B., and Tucker, C. "Exploring the Relation of Economic and Political Conditions with Refusal Rates to a Government Survey." *Journal of Official Statistics*, 1999, *15*(2), 167–184.

Kalton, G., Kasprzyk, D., and McMillen, D. B. "Nonsampling Errors in Panel Surveys." In D. Kaspryzk, G. Duncan, G. Kalton, and M. P. Singh (eds.), *Panel Surveys*. New York: Wiley, 1989.

Laurie, H., Smith, R., and Scott, L. "Strategies for Reducing Nonresponse in a Longitudinal Panel Survey." *Journal of Official Statistics*, 1999, *15*(2), 269–282.

McCarthy, J. S., and Beckler, D. G. "An Analysis of the Relationship Between Survey Burden and Non-response: If We Bother Them More, Are They Less Cooperative?" Paper presented at the International Conference on Survey Non-response, Portland, Oregon, October 1999.

Sharp, L. M., and Frankel, J. "Respondent Burden: A Test of Some Common Assumptions." *Public Opinion Quarterly*, 1983, *47*(1), 36–53.

Sosdian, C. P., and Sharp, L. M. "Nonresponse in Mail Surveys: Access Failure or Respondent Resistance." *Public Opinion Quarterly*, 1980, *44*(3), 396–402.

Steeh, C. G. "Trends in Nonresponse Rates, 1952–1979." *Public Opinion Quarterly*, 1981, *59*, 66–77.

STEPHEN R. PORTER *is director of institutional research at Wesleyan University.*

MICHAEL E. WHITCOMB *is assistant director of institutional research at Wesleyan University.*

WILLIAM H. WEITZER *is senior associate provost and dean of continuing studies at Wesleyan University.*

Although time and resource intensive, longitudinal studies offer the ability to examine the direction and magnitude of causal relationships that cannot be accomplished through cross-sectional design.

Conducting Longitudinal Studies

Karen W. Bauer

Educational researchers are required to possess multiple skills, including knowledge of research methods and design. Whereas cross-sectional design gathers data at only one "snapshot" point in time, allowing the researcher to examine differences by age, educational level, gender, or other characteristics, the longitudinal design enables the researcher to collect data, either from the same individuals or from a similar group at two or more points. Due to an increased interest in examining student change related to college attendance, the longitudinal method appears to be in a cycle of high interest. Although longitudinal studies provide some challenges, the researcher may want or need to study individual change in behaviors or attitudes over time and thus may want to choose and implement a longitudinal study.

Longitudinal, cohort, panel, or *time series studies* are most helpful in the study of individual variations in characteristics or traits and offer the opportunity to examine growth curves. Some authors use the term *longitudinal* to refer to both cohort and panel designs, while some purists prefer to use *longitudinal* to refer to panel studies only. *Time series* is a term used to cover a wide variety of models that analyze behavior over time. In psychological and educational research, many longitudinal studies focus on intraindividual change or on group differences in intraindividual change (Nesselroade and Baltes, 1979). Time series designs nicely accommodate the study of change. Likely the most familiar longitudinal studies in postsecondary education are the National Education Longitudinal Studies (NELS) of the National Center for Education Statistics (2002a), the Recent College Graduates study (National Center for Education Statistics, 2002b), and the more recent Baccalaureate and Beyond Longitudinal Study (National Center for Education Statistics, 2002c). Longitudinal analyses of change over time for college students are also becoming more frequent at research centers such as

NEW DIRECTIONS FOR INSTITUTIONAL RESEARCH, no. 121, Spring 2004 © Wiley Periodicals, Inc.

the Higher Education Research Institute at the University of California–Los Angeles and the Center for Postsecondary Research and Planning at Indiana University.

Cohort analysis as a research method was developed by demographers and originally applied to the study of fertility (Glenn, 1977). The first periodic collection of census data occurred in Quebec, Canada, from 1665 until 1754, and long-term studies of childhood development were frequent in the United States after World War I (Menard, 1991). In its broadest sense, cohort analysis is a technique of choice to provide insight into the effects of human aging and the nature of social, cultural, and political change. Nesselroade and Baltes (1979) discuss some of the varying perceptions of this design, but they ultimately believe that the one criterion—repeated investigation over time—must be present. They offer this working definition: "longitudinal methodology involves repeated time-ordered observation of an individual or individuals with the goal of identifying processes and causes of intra-individual change and of inter-individual patterns of intra-individual change in behavioral development" (p. 7).

Cohorts used in social science research usually consist of individuals who experience a common set of significant life events within a particular period. A *birth cohort* designates those who are born within a similar period; a *college* or *class cohort* may signify a group of college students who all matriculated during the same fall term. *Panel* studies are similar to cohort studies except that the same individuals are studied at two or more points in time. Panel studies thus allow the researcher to account for individual change. A cohort analysis, conversely, aggregates data across all members of the cohort, thus excluding the opportunity to include individual variance.

Researchers involved in aging research also turn to *retrospective reports*—respondents' cognitive recollections of their behavior, attitudes, and affective states at earlier times. Some researchers shy away from this method, knowing that respondents' recall may be inaccurate and that perceptions of earlier states may be confounded with later behaviors or attitudes. A robust *mixed design* would include facets of both cross-sectional and longitudinal designs (Cohen and Manion, 1980; Nesselroade and Baltes, 1979), but higher education resources usually do not encourage this.

Longitudinal Designs

Menard (1991) delineates four types of longitudinal designs, as shown in Figure 6.1. In each diagram, the horizontal dimension represents a period (month, year, decade) when data are collected, and the vertical dimension represents the cases for which data are collected (that is, the population or sample). In the *total population design,* the full population is measured in each period of the design. Due to changes such as birth, death, or dropout from the institution, the cases are not identical from one period to the next. When the periods are short, however, the majority of

Figure 6.1. Four Major Longitudinal Designs

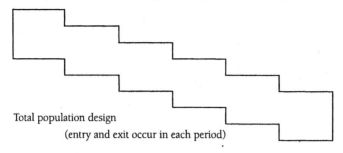

Total population design
   (entry and exit occur in each period)

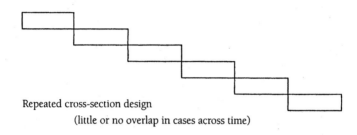

Repeated cross-section design
   (little or no overlap in cases across time)

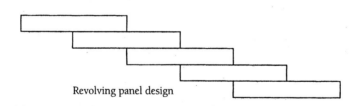

Revolving panel design

	Time 1	Time 2	Time 3	Time 4	Time 5	Time 6
Cohort 1						
Cohort 2						
Cohort 3						
Cohort 4						

Longitudinal panel design
(multiple cohort design)

cases are the same. This design enables the researcher to examine group change or trends.

In the *repeated cross-sectional design,* the researcher draws independent probability samples at each measurement period. Each sample includes different cases, but the cases across samples should be as comparable as possible. Comparisons of cohort data from the College Student Experiences Questionnaire (CSEQ) (Kuh and Vesper, 1997), the Cooperative Institutional Research Program and Your First College Year Survey from the Higher Educational Research Institute (Astin, 1998; Astin, Sax, and Avalos, 1999; Koch and Nelson, 1999; Sax and others, 2002), the National Survey of Youth, and some of the Monitoring the Future Studies (Menard, 1991) are examples of the repeated cross-sectional design (Menard, 1991). The major disadvantage of the repeated cross-sectional design is its inability to study developmental patterns within a cohort and to examine causal relationships. However, this design does enable the researcher to examine aggregate trends during one period and to replicate cross-sectional results across periods. For example, Kuh and Vesper (1997) examined responses from two different but comparable groups of first- and second-year students from 1990 and 1994, and Kojaltic and Kuh (2001) examined responses from several groups of CSEQ responders from 1984 through 1997. Kuh and Vesper found increases in student-faculty interactions at baccalaureate institutions between 1990 and 1994. Due to the nature of the cohorts having different respondents from several institutions, they were not, however, able to account for individual student differences (such as ability) nor for institutional context variables such as curricular requirements, administrative leadership, and potential changes in rewards for faculty engagement with students outside the classroom.

The *revolving panel design* collects data on a sample of cases for a specified measurement period, then drops some subjects, who are replaced with new subjects. The revolving panel design allows for repeated measurement in prospective studies and is helpful when cohort mortality is expected to be high. The retention of some individuals over a short period allows for examination of individual change, while replacement of the subsample permits analysis of long-term aggregate change. The National Crime Survey is an example of a revolving panel design (Menard, 1991). Households are selected for inclusion in this study by probability sampling, interviewed seven times over a three-year period, then dropped from the sample and replaced by newly selected households. In the analysis, household is the unit of analysis and allows for examination of short-term victimization within households and for long- and short-term aggregate rates of victimization.

The *longitudinal panel* is likely the most familiar design. Ideally, the exact same set of cases are used in each period, although attrition through death or other case discontinuance is likely. To help with subject mortality, longitudinal panel designs often include multiple cohorts and thus offer the most robust set of analyses. Multiple cohort panel designs enable analysis of age, period, and cohort effects; description of developmental and historical change; analysis of temporal order events; and causal analysis. The NELS (National Center for Education Statistics, 2002a), Baccalaureate and Beyond (National Center for Education Statistics, 2002b), some analyses from the Your First Year College studies (Sax and others, 2002), and the University of Delaware's Academic Experiences Study (Bauer, 2002; Bauer, Bennett, Shahid, and Wood, forthcoming) are examples of the longitudinal panel design. This design offers the widest range of potential analyses. The Baccalaureate and Beyond study will follow 1993 baccalaureate degree completers for approximately twelve years, examining graduate school, job search activities, teacher certification status, loan repayment status, and community service. The University of Delaware's Academic Experiences Study was used to examine intraindividual change in cognitive skills, changes in college activities from freshman to senior year (Bauer, 2001), and the relationship between change in personality typology and change in critical thinking (Bauer and Liang, forthcoming; DiLorenzo, Shahid, and Bauer, 2002). Data from the National Youth Survey (Menard, 1991) have been used, among other uses, to examine period trends in illegal behavior; to separate age, period, and cohort effects in drug use and other illegal behaviors; and to test and replicate a theoretical model of adolescence behavior.

Advantages and Disadvantages of the Longitudinal Design

There are advantages and disadvantages to both cross-sectional and longitudinal designs. In general, cross-sectional designs are less expensive, can produce findings more quickly, suffer from fewer control effects, and usually can include more subjects in the design for a given budget. The strengths of the longitudinal design, however, are the weaknesses of cross-sectional design (Cohen and Manion, 1980). The greatest advantage of longitudinal studies, as mentioned earlier, is the ability to identify individual variations in growth or to establish causal relationships between variables. Collection of data on individuals at three or more points enables powerful statistical modeling techniques, and the precision with which parameters of growth can be estimated improves with each additional wave of data (Willet, Singer, and Martin, 1998). Although cohort mortality can be a concern, the researcher can refine strategies to reduce nonresponse (Laurie, Smith, and Scott, 1999). For example, the NELS earn average response rates above 90 percent through preannouncements, multiple postal-return questionnaires, and telephone interviews. The University of Delaware's Academic Experiences Study achieved an average response rate of 89 percent for waves two through four due to a combination of e-mail and telephone contacts combined with small incentive awards and student-researcher rapport.

According to Cohen and Manion (1980), additional advantages to the longitudinal design include no reliance on self-reported retrospective data, no duplication of information (background demographic data in particular need to be collected only once and can save interview time and cost), the flexibility of adding new variables after the first data collection, and the accumulation of a large number of variables, often not possible in cross-sectional designs. Although Sikkel (1990) argues that recall errors can be corrected through a model-based estimator, other researchers prefer responses based on present-tense information. An added benefit is the ability to include new questionnaire items, especially if the longitudinal study examines cognitive reasoning or another construct that is harder to ascertain through one or two items. The researcher may learn of an instrument or series of items after the first wave of interviews has been completed. Although it won't be possible to examine change from point one, variables included after the first wave can still be included, and if at least three waves follow, change can still be examined over time. Through the University of Delaware's Academic Experiences Study, we learned of a measure of cognitive reasoning after the first wave of data collection was completed. We chose to include the measure beginning with the second wave and included it for the remaining three years (Bauer, Bennett, Shahid, and Wood, forthcoming).

Following the earlier discussion it is desirable to consider a longitudinal study when

- The stated objectives require measurement of individual change over time.
- A causal relationship can be postulated between an earlier and subsequent event.
- The measurement of traits, characteristics, or events proposed are meaningful and of reasonable validity.
- Results of the study will permit generalization.
- The analytic technique proposed will permit the exploration of the data gathered at intermediate stages as well as at end of inquiry.

Despite the advantages of longitudinal design, there are some concerns that must be considered. In addition to the time-consuming nature of longitudinal studies, the disadvantages of such designs include the possibility of selective sampling, participant survival and dropout, test-retest effects, and generation effects. These sources of error can affect the internal or external validity of the study. Because of the repeating nature of participation in a longitudinal study, cohort or panel studies often are not representative of the full population. For example, researchers may choose only full-time students in a particular major or discipline. As students change majors, it may not be possible to generalize findings to the major or discipline due to the small number of students remaining. In addition, it is possible that students who volunteer for a longitudinal study are biased in some way, perhaps more motivated or more conforming. Baltes (1968) reports that subjects who volunteer for longitudinal studies tend to be of a higher-than-average intelligence and socioeconomic status.

The concern of selective survival and nonresponse (or dropout) applies to both cross-sectional and longitudinal designs but can be compounded with multiple data collections. If Birren (1959) is correct, then "cohort 'survivors' may be, for example, taller or shorter, brighter or duller, happier or unhappier than their non-surviving cohort" (p. 150). If losses to the longitudinal design occur, they may threaten the ability to generalize data to a larger population, and thus minimize the value of the empirical study.

The concern of test effects is also noted with longitudinal studies but can be addressed by including a control group or statistical control in the analysis (such as covariates). When the period between waves is approximately one year or more, it is unlikely that test-retest effects will be a significant factor.

Wall and Williams (1970) remind us that the passage of time may lead to change in hypotheses or research questions. The longer the inquiry is, the more likely it is that some external change will occur that could diminish the value of the data collected. Can institutional leaders wait two to four years to see the final results? In some cases, yes, but in others, policy and programmatic change cannot wait that long.

Finally, concern about generation effects as a source of error can threaten the external validity of the longitudinal study. Because of the nature of the longitudinal design, the age effect of the study is generation specific. Findings from the longitudinal study represent results only for the age of individuals in the study and cannot be generalized to other age groups. For the researcher in an institution with a homogeneous population (such as traditional-age middle-class students), this may not be a concern. For the researcher in an institution with a wide variety of ages, the inclusion of a representative number of students across all age groups would be necessary in order to minimize generation effects. For a more detailed discussion of age effects, the reader is encouraged to review Baltes (1968) and Schaie (1965).

The Distinction Between Age, Period, and Time Effects

When considering a longitudinal research project, it is important to understand the distinction between age effects, period effects, and time effects. Researchers may find differences that appear to be related to age; however, they must be mindful of age-related differences measured through cross-sectional methods compared to those measured through longitudinal methods. In a cross-sectional design, for example, the cognitive differences between twenty- and thirty-year-olds may be interpreted as differences between two birth cohorts at one particular time. When cognitive differences are measured longitudinally, differences may be interpreted as developmental within a cohort that occurs over a period of time. Scott Menard (1991) offers examples of potential interpretive errors. Suppose the researcher wants to test the hypothesis that people become more politically conservative as they grow older. He or she might develop and administer a survey to respondents of different ages and compare the responses of older and younger respondents. If the responses differ between the groups, the researcher might conclude that the older respondents are politically more conservative than the younger respondents. There is, however, an alternate hypothesis: that the older respondents were simply more conservative throughout their lives and the younger respondents may remain more liberal as they grow older. Thus, the cross-sectional differences by age may be confused with differences that result not from age but from effects of membership in different birth cohorts.

In addition to the potential error in interpretation just described, there is also the possibility that historical events may affect behavior or attitudes. In the same example, if the researcher surveyed a cohort of similarly aged individuals over a period of years and found more conservative responses in subsequent administrations, he or she might conclude that conservatism increases with age. Indeed, that may be the case, but the researcher must also consider that contemporary events may have substantially affected individual attitudes, leading to more conservative answers over time. Thus conservative attitudes are not simply a function of increased age but the result of societal and intrapersonal events encountered over time. The astute researcher will realize that no one method is perfect, and these examples emphasize that point. The research design should be chosen in light of specific research questions developed for the project at hand, awareness of the advantages and disadvantages of both longitudinal and cross-sectional methods, and acknowledgment of the interpretive errors that may result from each.

Causal Relationships

One of the greatest benefits of the longitudinal design is the ability to determine a causal relationship between variables. To establish such a relationship between two or more variables, three criteria are essential: the variables in question must co-vary, the relationship must not be attributable to other variables, and the supposed cause must precede or be simultaneous with the effect of time (Menard, 1991). In most instances, it is possible to determine the first two criteria through cross-sectional analyses, but the longitudinal design is needed for the third.

A linear panel analysis can examine reciprocal causal influences nicely. An example might look for relationships among student participation in specific college activities (such as marching band, student government, or undergraduate research), college success as defined by grade-point average (GPA), and critical thinking. A series of models are calculated, with each variable in turn considered as a dependent variable, and all variables measured prior to the time of the 'dependent variable (this can be a lagged endogenous variable such as the dependent variable measured at a previous time) are included as predictors of the dependent variable. In this analysis, the possibility that each variable has some effect on every other variable can be examined in a way that is impossible with cross-sectional data. The inclusion of the lagged endogenous variable in the equation helps control for the effects of extraneous (unmeasured) variables and provides a fairly conservative test for the existence of a causal relationship (Menard, 1991).

Attrition in Longitudinal Studies

As mentioned earlier, attrition or cohort mortality is one of the greatest challenges for longitudinal studies. Geographic mobility, enrollment dropout, and panel fatigue contribute to attrition. If high attrition rates occur, generalization may not be possible; thus the researcher should include procedures to minimize nonresponse. Laurie, Smith, and Scott (1999) delineate important points, including quality control at all stages of the longitudinal study, a specified number of follow-up visits or telephone contact or both, and brevity in size and clarity of survey content. Based on their British Household Panel Study (BHPS) (Laurie, Smith, and Scott, 1999), these authors note that strategies for specific fieldwork, panel maintenance, tracking, and refusal conversations are important. For best results, quality control must be implemented in all phases. In the BHPS, where possible, the same interviewers were assigned to the same households at each wave. A side benefit of keeping the same interviewers is that rapport with respondents can be built. In addition, BHPS interviewers were required to make a minimum of six calls to each address before declaring the household a noncontact. Another aspect of quality control requires planning and implementation of a database or other computer-driven system to ensure accurate and up-to-date records on each respondent. If the respondents are likely to be moving (important to know for longitudinal studies such as the Baccalaureate and Beyond or household panel studies), this is an important feature to consider during initial planning. In most instances, researchers must rely on the goodwill of respondents to share new addresses or other contact information; interviewers who have developed rapport with and who have knowledge of the respondent and his or her circumstances will be most successful in achieving contact. In the BHPS, respondents with different interviewers were 20 percent more likely to discontinue (Laurie, Smith, and Scott, 1999). Finally, strategies for minimizing refusal are also important to consider in the initial planning stages. The wording of cover letters and e-mail introductions and the first words spoken during an in-person or phone interview are critical. Some refusals to participate occur for each wave, while other refusals may occur for the total study. Laurie, Smith, and Scott have achieved success by explaining the purpose of the survey more fully or by pointing out each respondent's importance as an individual (and perhaps irreplaceable) member of the cohort.

Practical Considerations in Longitudinal Studies

From a practical standpoint, several important issues must be considered. These include determining if a longitudinal design is the best approach for the research questions under review, total time allotments the researcher can devote to the study, and budget.

Appropriateness of the Longitudinal Study. First decide if a longitudinal study is right for the research questions under review. Research questions guide the design of the study. Do the questions require the use of a longitudinal method or perhaps a mixed design that includes some cross-sectional data as well? Generally cross-sectional analyses are less resource intensive but cannot examine developmental, intraindividual change. Consider the advantages of longitudinal design and decide how the threats to validity will be handled.

Overall Planning and Organization. Because of the compact time frame of a single cross-sectional survey, it is important to plan for all stages of the project, including design and pilot testing of the instrument or instruments, training of staff, data collection, coding, analysis, and reporting of the results. Longitudinal studies pose the additional challenges of retaining staff (often all or part are graduate students), the resources needed to encourage continued respondent participation, and the skills necessary to complete partial analyses throughout the study. Ideally a strong and complete strategy and timeline should be in place at the beginning of the longitudinal study. It is possible, however, that the best-laid plans will go awry, and thus the researcher must consider and plan for potential changes. For example, it may be necessary to postpone the measurement occasions for some subjects or to develop very high response rates for wave two following a larger than expected mortality rate after the first wave. Longitudinal designs are even more at risk for cohort mortality than cross-sectional designs. Gorard (2001) offers a clear discussion on issues to consider regarding sample size, and Dillman (2000) describes strategies for high response rates. One strategy for increasing response rates is to use incentives. If respondent investment is very high, an incentive may not be necessary, but in most longitudinal studies they are. Berry and Kanouse (1987) and Berk, Mathiowetz, Ward, and White (1987) found that prepaid incentives did increase response rates but a promised incentive did not. In the University of Delaware's Academic Experiences Study a cash award was given as well as the opportunity to participate in a random drawing for several postsurvey awards. Based on the nonverbal responses observed and the anecdotal comments received from students in this study, the incentives were a significant factor contributing to high response rates.

Budgeting. Because of the personnel costs, the techniques needed to maintain contact with subjects over time, the costs of incentives, and the need for detailed documentation of data, the time and funding required for longitudinal studies are much greater than those required for cross-sectional designs. A careful analysis of all resources is needed. No matter how advanced the researcher is (that is, has completed many cross-sectional survey studies), the researcher doing his or her first longitudinal study may not know how to budget for unexpected changes in personnel or realize the time involved in data documentation. A good rule of thumb (passed on anecdotally by colleagues) is to double the time that was originally anticipated for completion of tasks related to the longitudinal study, especially data analysis. Increases in time will also lead to heightened funding needs.

Gaining and Maintaining Cooperation. Students in higher education receive many solicitations for survey information. Response rates for the first contact are a challenge, with many college student surveys averaging a 30 percent to 50 percent response rate. Longitudinal researchers have the added burden of retaining students over two or more waves of surveys. For these reasons, it is critical that researchers plan to retain the same interviewers or individuals who will have contact with the respondents, and to disclose fully and clearly why students' responses are valued, how the data will be used, and how the respondents will receive follow-up findings. Once initial participation is achieved, high response rates for longitudinal studies can be achieved with continued contact (personal face-to-face is best) and reiteration of the purposes and intent of the data collection. Especially within the longitudinal design, incentives can contribute to increased continuation. According to Dillman (2000, p. 27), today "high response rates require more intensive efforts." Consider incentives that are valued by the population; perhaps it is a small cash award or an item such as a bicycle or laptop computer. Perhaps complementary parking in a highly desired area on campus is valued. Incentives can be used to encourage participation and can also reward and encourage thoughtful and accurate completion of instruments.

Keeping Senior Leaders Informed Throughout the Data Collection Process. Related to gaining and maintaining the cooperation of student participants, it is important to keep senior-level campus officials informed throughout the study. For example, if a four-year study is under way, report the findings after the first and second years to inform others about the descriptive data from this early period, and present some initial findings for change in growth. A note of caution: before sharing preliminary findings, always consider the nature of findings in relation to your total project, and share only those findings that make sense in the context of your research questions, or be certain to include caveats about the nature of initial findings. For example, if increases in critical thinking are hypothesized over a four-year period, changes may not be detected after one or two years or may actually decrease. Reporting the decrease may erroneously leave some readers with the impression that critical thinking does not improve over time.

Determining the Sample Size. Due to the likelihood of respondent mortality and the likely need for subgroup analyses, it is important to begin with the largest sample possible. Constraints related to management of the subjects will likely restrict the sample size. If subject discontinuance (mortality) is expected to be substantial, then one may want to consider a revolving panel or multiple cohort panel design. Hoogendorn and Sikkel (1998) also discuss the value of split panel and rotating panel designs as well as the quota sampling technique to keep panel size constant over time.

Data Checking, Coding, and Documentation. While checking, coding, and documentation are important concepts for any study, they are particularly important for longitudinal studies. Personnel changes and failed memories over a period of years can and likely will happen, thus detailed documentation becomes extremely important. Careful thought should be given to how data will be coded, considering that the same measure may be used again. In panel studies, data should be tied to the individual respondent so that subsequent data can be added to individual records. If there are a large number of variables, it will be helpful to produce a codebook or data dictionary.

Determining the Appropriate Analyses. Along with their design, longitudinal studies can be complex and require thoughtful planning for data analysis. Linear dependence and autocorrelation of variables are possible and must be addressed. Mason, Mason, Winsborough, and Poole (1973) believe that linear dependence from age effects, period effects, or birth cohort effects can be addressed through the use of dummy variables in a standard regression analysis.

The astute researcher must also consider how to address change, especially when examining developmental questions such as change in content-specific skill or broader constructs such as critical thinking. Longitudinal studies can yield raw change scores or residual change scores. Raw change scores are the simple difference between a variable at two time points ($X_2 - X_1$). Residual change is obtained when the variable Y_2 is first regressed on Y_1 to obtain a predicted or expected value for Y_2. The expected or predicted value thus depends on the value of Y_1 as well as on the values of the intercept (the expected value of Y_2 when Y_1 is zero) and the slope between Y_2 and Y_1. Residual gain is the difference between the actual value of Y_2 and the predicted value of Y_2.

There is debate among researchers about the appropriateness of raw gain versus residual scores. In their classic article, Cronbach and Furby (1970) argue against the use of raw scores (they have too much measurement error and lower reliability can lead to false conclusions) and for the use of residual scores. Plewis (1985), however, argues that measurement error from residual scores is often similar to that from raw scores. Kessler and Greenberg (1981) suggest a different approach—use lagged endogenous variables to examine change. One should review these articles as well as a brief but helpful discussion in Pascarella and Terenzini (1991, see Appendix) prior to beginning analyses.

In addition to considering change scores, it is important to remember that relationships between variables may change over time, and it may be appropriate to test for these differences. The use of repeated measures analysis of variance or another general linear model can enable the researcher to examine change scores in a way that accounts for the baseline or first-wave measure. The most popular new method for the analysis of longitudinal data (especially for samples with more than two hundred participants) is Hierarchical Linear Modeling (HLM). Porter and Umbach (2000, 2001) include several good discussions of the use of HLM in the educational research setting.

Need for Confidentiality, Informed Consent, and Human Subjects Approval. Although there is some debate about the need for human subjects approval when data are collected for institutional improvement, it is wise to receive both individual informed consent and institutional human subjects approval for any longitudinal study. In addition, confidentiality is very important to the success of the study. If students do not perceive their information to be held in confidence, they are likely to drop out or refuse to participate. Although respondents need to include some sort of identifier on each measure and at every point of data collection, it is possible to maintain anonymity by replacing students' identification from the original source with a code number. There are several good resources that further delineate research with human subjects, including the Department of Education. For a brief history and background on human subjects policy, see http://www.udel.edu/OVPR/humans/history.html, and for more information about human subjects guidelines, see http://www.med.umich.edu/irbmed/FederalDocuments/hhs/HHS45CFR46.html.

Practical Advice for Educational Researchers Who Want to Consider Conducting a Longitudinal Study

One of the most exciting and intellectually challenging tasks for the educational researcher is the design, implementation, and analysis of new research projects. The addition of the longitudinal design to one's repertoire is important, and the implementation of a successful longitudinal study is hard work that requires flexibility, patience, and tenacity on the part of the researcher.

Acquisition of adequate budget and personnel is essential to make the longitudinal study a success. It is important to ensure funding support not only for the primary researcher but also for graduate assistants and secretaries who can provide much-needed assistance with survey mailings, interviews, and telephone and e-mail reminders to participants; help with data collection (especially if data are collected in more than one location at a time); and assist with data coding, entry, and analysis. As mentioned earlier, it is easy to underestimate the amount of time needed for all tasks in a longitudinal study, so it is essential to give considerable thought to all aspects of the project as the budget and timeline are created.

Along with complicated budgets comes the potential for complex statistical analyses. In general, the more numerous the data collection points, the more advanced the analysis will need to be. Advanced statistical techniques such as HLM can offer powerful ways to analyze the data for intraindividual change. Related to complicated design, analyses with longitudinal data sets will take longer than might initially be expected. The volume of data and potential interaction among variables may prompt the need for unexpected intermediate analyses, for additional analyses that were not originally anticipated, or for both. In the early planning stages, list the variables that will be received throughout the study to look for duplicate or unnecessary data.

Despite the challenges, researchers should consider doing longitudinal studies. Examination of individual behavior and attitudes over time is fascinating, of interest to many higher education stakeholders, and highly important to the policies and programs offered within higher education institutions. While cross-sectional designs are informative and good for descriptive information obtained from a snapshot point in time, the study of individual change is best explored through longitudinal design. At the completion of the long process, you will feel not only excited with your findings but also internally rewarded for accomplishing an important research project.

References

Astin, A. W. "The Changing American College Student: Thirty-Year Trends, 1966–1996." *Review of Higher Education,* 1998, *21*(2), 115–135.

Astin, A. W., Sax, L. J., and Avalos, J. "Long-Term Effects of Volunteerism During the Undergraduate Years." *Review of Higher Education,* 1999, 22(2), 187–202.

Baltes, P. B. "Longitudinal and Cross-Sectional Sequences in the Study of Age and Generation Effects." *Human Development,* 1968, *11,* 145–171.

Baltes, P. B., and Nesselroade, J. R. "History and Rationale of Longitudinal Research." In J. R. Nesselroade and P. B. Baltes (eds.), *Longitudinal Research in the Study of Behavior and Development.* New York: Academic Press, 1979.

Bauer, K. W. "The Effect of Participation in Undergraduate Research on Critical Thinking and Reflective Judgment." Paper presented at the Association for Institutional Research Forum, Long Beach, Calif., May 2001.

Bauer, K. W. "Two Major Assessment Efforts Under Way at the University of Delaware." *Assessment Update,* 2002, *14*(6), 5–7.

Bauer, K. W., Bennett, J. B., Shahid, A., and Wood, P. "A Longitudinal Assessment of Undergraduate Research." *Research in Higher Education,* forthcoming.

Bauer, K. W. and Liang, Q. "The Effect of Personality and Precollege Characteristics on First Year Activities and Academic Performance." *Journal of College Student Development,* forthcoming.

Berk, M. L., Mathiowetz, N. A., Ward, E. P., and White, A. A. "The Effect of Prepaid and Promised Incentives: Results of a Controlled Experiment." *Journal of Official Statistics,* 1987, 3(4), 449–457.

Berry, S. H., and Kanouse, D. E. "Physician Response to a Mailed Survey: An Experiment in Timing of Payment." *Public Opinion Quarterly,* 1987, 51, 102–116.

Birren, J. E. *Handbook of Aging and the Individual.* Chicago: University of Chicago Press, 1959.

Cohen, L., and Manion, L. *Research Methods in Education.* London: Croon Helm, 1980.

Cronbach, L., and Furby, L. "How Should We Measure Change—or Should We?" *Psychological Bulletin,* 1970, 74, 68–80.

Dillman, D. *Mail and Internet Surveys.* New York: Wiley, 2000.

DiLorenzo, T., Shahid, A., and Bauer, K. "The Effect of Personality and Academic and Social Activities on Critical Thinking and Reasoning." Unpublished paper, University of Delaware, 2002.

Glenn, N. D. *Cohort Analysis.* Thousand Oaks, Calif.: Sage, 1977.

Gorard, S. *Quantitative Methods in Educational Research: The Role of Numbers Made Easy.* New York: Continuum Press, 2001.

Hoogendorn, A. W., and Sikkel, D. "Response Burden and Panel Attrition." *Journal of Official Statistics,* 1998, 14(2), 189–205.

Kessler, R. C., and Greenberg, D. F. *Linear Panel Analysis: Models of Quanttative Change.* New York: Wiley, 1981.

Koch, G., and Nelson, K. "Assessing Trends in Student Attitudes Using CIRP Data, 1985–1994." *Journal of the First-Year Experience & Students in Transition,* 1999, 11(1), 7–24.

Kojaltic, M., and Kuh, G. "A Longitudinal Assessment of College Student Engagement in Good Practices in Undergraduate Education." *Higher Education,* 2001, 42(3), 351–371.

Kuh, G., and Vesper, N. "A Comparison of Student Experiences with Good Practices in Undergraduate Education Between 1990 and 1994." *Review of Higher Education,* 1997, 21, 43–61.

Laurie, H., Smith, R., and Scott, L. "Strategies for Reducing Nonresponse in a Longitudinal Panel Survey." *Journal of Official Statistics,* 1999, 15(2), 269–282.

Mason, K. O., Mason, W. M., Winsborough, H. H., and Poole, W. K. "Some Methodological Issues in Cohort Analysis of Archival Data." *American Sociological Review,* 1973, 41, 242–258.

Menard, S. *Longitudinal Research.* Quantitative Applications in the Social Sciences, paper no. 07–076. Newbury Park, Calif.: Sage, 1991.

National Center for Education Statistics. "High School and Beyond: Overview." Washington, D.C.: National Center for Education Statistics, 2002a. [http://nces.ed.gov/surveys/hsb]. Access date: Nov. 15, 2002.

National Center for Education Statistics. "Recent College Graduates: Overview." Washington, D.C.: National Center for Education Statistics, 2002b. [http://nces.ed.gov/surveys/rcg]. Access date: Nov. 15, 2002.

National Center for Education Statistics. "Baccalaureate and Beyond: Overview." Washington, D.C.: National Center for Education Statistics, 2002c. [http://nces.ed.gov/surveys/b&b]. Access date: Nov. 15, 2002.

Nesselroade, J. R., and Baltes, P. B. *Longitudinal Research in the Study of Behavior and Development.* New York: Academic Press, 1979.

Pascarella, E., and Terenzini, P. *How College Affects Students.* San Francisco: Jossey-Bass, 1991.

Plewis, I. *Analyzing Change: Measurement and Explanation Using Longitudinal Data.* Chichester, England: Wiley, 1985.

Porter, S. R., and Umbach, P. D. "Analyzing Faculty Workload Data Using Multilevel

Modeling." Paper presented at 40th Annual Association for Institutional Research Forum, Cincinnati, Ohio, May 21–24, 2000.

Porter, S. R., and Umbach, P. D. "Analyzing Faculty Workload Data Using Multilevel Modeling." *Research in Higher Education,* 2001, *42,* 171–196.

Sax, L., Keup, J., Gilmartin S., Stolzenberg, E., and Harper, C. "Findings from the 2002 Administration of Your First College Year (YFCY): National Aggregates." Los Angeles: Higher Education Research Institute, University of California, 2002. [http://www.gseis.ucla.edu/heri/yfcy/yfcy_report_year3.pdf]. Access date: Jan. 21, 2004.

Schaie, K. W. "A General Model for the Study of Development Problems." *Psychological Bulletin,* 1965, *64,* 208–215.

Sikkel, D. "Retrospective Questions and Group Differences." *Journal of Official Statistics,* 1990, *6*(2), 165–177.

Wall, W. D., and Williams, H. C. *Longitudinal Studies and the Social Sciences.* London: Heinemann Press, 1970.

Willet, J.B., Singer, J. D., and Martin, N. "The Design and Analysis of Longitudinal Studies of Development and Psychopathology in Context: Statistical Models and Methodological Recommendations." *Development and Psychopathology,* 1998, *10,* 395–426.

KAREN W. BAUER *is director of institutional research and associate professor at the Institute of Higher Education, University of Georgia.*

This chapter describes the different types of paper and electronic surveys currently available and their costs and benefits in terms of equipment and printing costs, demands on staff time, and ease of use.

Pros and Cons of Paper and Electronic Surveys

Stephen R. Porter

As discussed in Chapters One and Two, researchers today have several different options to choose from when conducting a survey, from the traditional paper-and-pencil surveys to technically sophisticated Web surveys with automatic question branching. Without knowing the advantages and disadvantages of these approaches, it becomes difficult to make an informed decision. As demands for surveys of students and faculty grow and institutional budgets tighten, knowing how to get the biggest bang for your survey research dollar is important for all institutional researchers.

Most institutional researchers use one of five types of surveys. Fill-in-the-blank (FITB) surveys, which use sheets of paper with check-off boxes and blank spaces for written responses, is the most familiar method of administering a survey. Two additional types of paper surveys have become more common because they are machine-scannable. The first is called an optical mark recognition survey (OMR), often referred to as a "bubble" survey because of the small circles that must be filled in to indicate particular responses. The second is referred to as an optical character recognition (OCR) survey. Each of these surveys appears similar to the other; the difference lies in how each is scanned. OMR survey scanners can read only markings such as bubbles. OCR surveys combine optical scanners and sophisticated text-recognition software, so these surveys can use not only bubbles but also check boxes. More important, the OCR software, similar to word processing, can read text written by the respondent and convert it into an electronic format similar to that provided by a word processor.

Finally, many researchers have adopted one of two types of electronic surveys. The first type is a survey sent via e-mail, either as text in the body of the e-mail itself or as an electronic attachment. The second type is the more familiar Web survey, an HTML form that is posted on a Web site, of which respondents are notified.

This chapter discusses the costs and benefits of each approach. It looks at six different aspects of survey administration: required equipment, survey development, transmission of the survey, data entry of responses, handling of open-ended questions, and overall project time. The technology in these areas is constantly changing, so the costs will also change. Thus the costs mentioned here should be taken only as ballpark figures; before making any decisions it would useful to contact several vendors to inquire about prices and capabilities.

Equipment

FITB surveys have the lowest equipment costs of the five approaches. For a basic survey, all that is required is a personal computer, word processing software, and a printer. For surveys with extensive graphics or color, a color copier may be required, or the copies of the survey must be created using a printing shop.

While the responses to completed FITB surveys must be hand-entered into a database, OMR and OCR surveys are optically scanned to create the survey response database. This requires two additional pieces of equipment: a scanner and scanning software. The scanner creates an optical image of each completed survey. The scanning software combines the survey template created by the researcher with the optical image of each completed survey and creates a database containing responses to the survey.

Scanner prices range from $500 to well over $5,000, depending on the features. In general, scanner costs are driven by the type of scanning (simplex, or one-sided, versus duplex, or two-sided), the speed at which a page is scanned, the size of the document feeder, the ability to scan color documents, and the ability to handle different sizes of paper. A large document feeder is necessary when processing large numbers of completed surveys. Feeding a thousand completed surveys through a scanner that accepts only twenty-five at a time can be quite time-consuming.

The main difference between the two types of scanning software is the ability to process the scanned image. Software for bubble surveys is generally limited in what it can process (whether a bubble has been filled in), while OCR software can scan and read entire paragraphs of written text. The latter types of systems are especially suited for surveys with open-ended questions.

There are several options for generating e-mail and Web surveys. The simplest e-mail survey can be a text e-mail or Microsoft Word document attached to an e-mail, with the results hand-entered into a database. Software can also be purchased that will send out and process e-mail surveys.

For Web surveys, you can purchase comprehensive systems that will allow you to design and post the survey on the Web, and the costs for these systems are rapidly decreasing as the technology changes and the market becomes more competitive. Alternatively, FrontPage or Cold Fusion software can be used to develop the HTML for a Web-based survey. These software packages can be purchased for less than $500.

The biggest difference between the do-it-all software for Web surveys and HTML software such as FrontPage lies in ease of use and flexibility. Software specifically designed to post surveys on the Web requires less technical skill than HTML software; conversely, programming the survey in HTML yourself generally allows more flexibility and complexity in terms of survey appearance and design. Web surveys generated from scratch may also be more easily combined with your institution's security system. For example, we generate our Web surveys using FrontPage, and our information technology group has developed a system that allows our surveys to be nested within the university's security system. This allows students and faculty to log into our surveys using their university ID and password and does not require us to assign unique IDs and passwords for every survey.

Bulk email software is also available for purchase, and simple shareware versions are available for free. The software can be used for e-mail surveys or to send e-mail notifications for Web surveys. This software makes it easy to send large numbers of e-mails notifying respondents of the survey location, as well as to personalize the salutation and other parts of the message. Such software also allows the researcher to send unique survey URLs to each respondent so that clicking on the URL automatically logs the respondent into the Web survey.

Survey Development

Survey development costs are generally lower for electronic surveys than for paper surveys. Printing costs for FITB and OCR surveys are generally the same, because the OCR software can process the typical FITB survey. Costs for OMR surveys can be substantial, especially if special survey forms must be ordered from a firm specializing in bubble surveys. In general, local copy shops can charge anywhere from five to twenty cents a page for a printed survey, depending on size and paper quality.

Costs for e-mail and Web surveys are in one sense free. These surveys are electronic and thus copies can be created easily on a computer. There can be hidden development costs, however, if there is no in-office expert who is familiar with the technology. The need to work with a liaison from the information technology office can increase the amount of time it takes to develop and administer the survey. Software packages designed specifically to generate and administer surveys can help avoid this issue.

Transmission

The main division in transmission costs is between paper and electronic surveys. With paper surveys, transmission costs include the costs of printing copies of the survey, copies of the cover letter, and copies of additional communications such as a prenotification letter and a reminder letter or postcard. In addition, the surveys and reminder letters require envelopes for mailing to the participants. Each survey mailing will also require a return envelope for the completed survey. For surveys of off-campus constituencies such as alumni, each communication will require postage, as will the return envelopes for the completed surveys. Finally, the survey mailings must be assembled (letters folded, envelopes stuffed, and so on). This will require either staff time or fees paid to a bulk mail firm. Note that although staff time is generally not a direct cost, an opportunity cost is involved with staff use for survey assemblage: every hour spent on mailings is an hour not spent on other research projects. Together these costs can be quite substantial. Even a short one- or two-page survey sent through campus mail could cost fifty cents or more per survey depending on the number of mailings.

Transmission costs for electronic surveys, on the other hand, are generally zero. Other than the staff time necessary for generating e-mails to members of the sample, there are no costs in sending e-mails. With bulk e-mail software, staff time can be kept to a minimum. Clearly this is one of the main advantages of electronic surveys. Substantial cost savings can occur with electronic surveys. The only downside is that valid e-mail addresses are necessary for the entire sample, and the researcher must be fairly certain that the e-mail addresses are being checked on a regular basis (see Chapter Two for a more detailed discussion).

Data Entry of Responses

One of the often overlooked costs of conducting a survey is the data entry of responses. FITB surveys require personnel to enter the individual survey responses into a database. This results in three types of costs that must be considered: personnel costs, either direct (for example, hiring a temporary worker) or indirect (opportunity costs of other projects not worked on); project time costs, because the time required for data entry increases the amount of time it takes to collect and analyze the data and present results to policymakers; and data entry error. Because they are entered by hand there will likely be errors in the data, unless the surveys are entered into a database by a second person and the two sets of data are compared. Each of these costs should be borne in mind when considering a particular method of survey administration.

Data entry for OMR surveys can vary. Some schools send their completed survey questionnaires to an external firm for scanning; this increases both monetary costs and project time. Survey scanning costs charged by external vendors can be substantial, with fees as high as fifty cents per survey, plus shipping and handling fees. Conversely, a purchased OMR scanner can be used for scanning.

Generally, OCR surveys are designed and scanned in-house. Here data entry can be quite rapid, because the survey database is created as each survey is scanned. The attributes of the scanner, however, determine how quickly scanning will take place. Like laser printers, cheaper scanners will generally be slower than more expensive ones.

There may be some scanning errors with both OMR and OCR surveys, but the extent will depend on the construction of the survey form, the capabilities of the scanner, and the quality of the software.

Data entry issues for electronic surveys vary. E-mail surveys can be problematic if the survey is sent within the e-mail. The e-mail is a text file and respondents may inadvertently insert or delete characters in the survey portion of the e-mail. When the email is returned, these stray characters can cause problems and may require editing out by hand. This problem can vary for attached surveys, depending on whether the attachment is a text file, HTML file, or word processing document. When considering e-mail survey software, vendors should be questioned about data entry performance.

Web surveys offer perhaps the simplest and quickest form of data entry. Such data entry is simple because it is done by the respondents; when the "submit" button in the HTML form is clicked, responses are saved to a survey database. This method is quickest because the data entry occurs almost in real time, just after the respondent finishes the survey. An additional advantage is that data entry errors are almost nonexistent (but HTML errors, such as wrong name-value tags, are possible).

Handling of Open-Ended Questions

Many surveys include either short open-ended answer options for questions (such as "other, please describe") or questions that are completely open-ended; that is, the respondent can answer the question only by writing one or more statements. These questions can provide a wealth of detail and insight into the survey topic, but this rich source of information comes at a price: it must be processed and analyzed. The general approach is to have two researchers read each comment and assign it a topic code; these codes can then be analyzed to provide summary information about the open-ended responses.

Although this coding process can be done by reading the written comments on paper surveys, it is much more efficient to use a qualitative software program such as N6 (formerly Nudist) to highlight and code respondent comments. Such software requires comments to be in an electronic format.

For FITB and OMR surveys, personnel must type the comments into an electronic database to be analyzed by qualitative software or for keyword searches. If a survey must be done on paper, OCR surveys have a clear advantage. OCR software can recognize and convert handwritten responses into an electronic format. While some errors do occur during processing, the software currently available is quite sophisticated and can read most handwriting.

Obviously electronic surveys also have an advantage here because the open-ended responses are typed by the respondent into an electronic form. Legibility of handwriting is not an issue as it is with paper surveys.

Project Time

From the preceding discussion we can see that paper surveys will most likely result in the longest project time. These surveys must be printed and transmitted to the respondent, a possibly lengthy process if the survey must be sent and returned through the mail. Data entry can also lengthen project time in the case of FITB surveys, and also with OMR surveys if they must be mailed offsite to a vendor for scanning. OCR surveys, conversely, promise fairly quick data entry, depending on the capabilities of the scanner.

Electronic surveys will usually have much shorter project times than paper surveys. There are no printing times to consider; once the survey has been created electronically it is ready for sending. Transmission and return times are almost instantaneous. In terms of project times, e-mail and Web surveys differ primarily in data entry. While the data from Web surveys is entered by the respondent via an HTML form, completed e-mail surveys must be processed by a software program that creates the survey database. Depending on the survey, this will take some time if the returned surveys must be corrected by hand for proper reading.

Conclusion

Despite the move toward electronic surveys, paper surveys will always play a role in institutional research, at least for the near future. Some populations may not be easily reached through the Web; in addition, there will always be the need to administer surveys in classrooms, a setting that usually requires the use of paper surveys.

From the previous discussion we can see that Web surveys appear to have the greatest benefits and lowest costs of the currently available alternatives. When faced with a situation where good e-mail addresses are available for the population under study, a researcher can save money with a Web survey by avoiding costs such as the purchase of scanning equipment, the printing of surveys, and postage, while at the same time reducing survey administration time and data entry errors. Web surveys seem especially useful for the current generation of college students, who are much more familiar with the Web and more likely to have and use e-mail compared with earlier generations.

Another benefit of Web surveys is that they may reduce the costs of filling out a survey. We know that the probability of survey response increases when we can decrease the cost to the respondent (see Chapter One of this volume); hence shorter surveys tend to have higher response rates than longer surveys. Given a Web survey and paper survey of similar length (especially paper bubble surveys), a Web survey may be quicker to fill out because respondents simply have to click their mouse to answer rather than spend time filling in bubbles with a pencil.

These reduced costs are also valuable for longitudinal surveys. Such surveys can be difficult to conduct because survey participation must be maintained for several iterations (see Chapter Six). Providing participants with a Web option may help to maintain participation. However, as Bauer discusses in her chapter, personal contact with participants is also necessary and may in fact lessen if surveys are administered via the Web.

Note that although Web surveys appear to be more cost-effective than paper surveys, we still face complicated choices when trying to decide on a particular mode of survey administration. For example, as discussed in Chapter Three, anonymity can be important for surveys on sensitive topics. Yet assuring respondents of anonymity on the Web can be difficult, because people can be suspicious about how much information is being recorded. Computer Internet Protocol addresses can be surreptitiously recorded by the researcher, for example (see the discussion of ethics in Chapter Two). Security also complicates the issue, because most Web surveys require respondents to log in to prevent multiple survey submissions by one respondent. Requiring a login with an institutional identification number makes anonymity impossible; respondents can be physically mailed a temporary identification number and password, but this mailing defeats the efforts to save costs by using surveys on the Web.

The ease of use and low costs of Web surveys can also be a disadvantage if the number of surveys administered at your institution increases. On the basis of conversations with colleagues at other institutions, it is clear that many schools conduct relatively few student surveys throughout the academic year due to a lack of budgetary and staff resources. Switching to Web surveys can make administering monthly, weekly, or even daily surveys a possibility for even the smallest institutional research office. Yet the analysis in Chapter Five indicates that multiple surveys do indeed cause survey fatigue. Switching from paper to Web surveys may save money, but at the same time it may also reduce the quality of the survey data due to increased surveying.

In sum, institutional researchers now have several options available for collecting information with surveys. Each option has both costs and benefits, and these may differ depending on the institution and the makeup of students and faculty. Being aware of the weaknesses of each approach can help researchers avoid problems when conducting surveys, and guide future decisions about software and hardware purchases.

STEPHEN R. PORTER *is director of institutional research at Wesleyan University.*

INDEX

Admitted Student Questionnaire, 55
Age effects, in longitudinal study, 81–82
Alcohol and drug research: data source for, 79; and response validity, 42
Alumni surveys, 5
Anderston, W. T., 54
Anonymity: and human subject review, 46; in longitudinal studies, 87; in sensitive-topic surveys, 42–43, 47–48
Antons, C. M., 6, 13, 65
Apodaca, R., 65
Aquilino, W., 42
Asiu, B. W., 6, 13, 65
Assessment, 5, 63–64
Astin, A. W., 78
Atrostic, B. K., 5, 65
Attrition, in longitudinal studies, 78–79, 81, 83–84
Avalos, J., 78

Baccalaureate and Beyond Longitudinal Study, 75, 79, 83
Baltes, P. B., 75, 76, 81
Baruch, Y., 5
Bates, N., 65
Bauer, K. W., 79, 80
Baumgartner, R., 11, 12, 13, 14, 15, 53, 55
Beckler, D. G., 66
Bennett, J. B., 79, 80
Berge, Z. L., 24, 27
Berk, M. L., 13, 53, 84
Berry, S. H., 13, 53, 84
Bers, T., 11
Birren, J. E., 81
Birth cohort, defined, 76
Blackwell, K., 10, 13
Blair, J., 53, 55
Bogen, K., 11
Bolstein, R., 13, 14, 51, 53, 55, 56
Bowers, A., 12
Bowker, D., 10, 23, 25, 26, 29, 30, 31
Bradshaw, C. C., 9
British Household Panel Study (BHPS), 83
Bryant, A. N., 26, 27
"Bubble" survey. See Optical mark recognition survey (OMR)
Burt, G., 5, 65

Carey, M. P., 42, 43
Carini, R. M., 9, 24, 26
Carson, C., 10, 13
Center for Postsecondary Research and Planning at Indiana University, 76
Childers, T. L., 11, 12, 13, 16, 53
Cho, H., 27
Church, A., 51, 52, 53
Church, A. H., 13
Cialdini, R. B., 7, 8, 15
Clark, J. R., 11, 14, 15
Cobanoglu, C., 9
Coding errors, and Web surveys, 24
Cohen, L., 76, 79, 80
Cohort analysis: defined, 75, 76; disadvantages of, 80–81
College Student Experiences Questionnaire (CSEQ), 66, 78
College/class cohort, defined, 76
Collins, M. P., 24, 27
Collins, R. L., 53
Confidentiality: in longitudinal studies, 87; in sensitive-topic surveys, 42–43, 47–48; in Web surveys, 27
Confidentiality statements, and survey participation, 14–15
Conradt, J., 10
Converse, J. M., 36
Cook, C., 13, 23, 31, 32, 53
Coomber, R., 25
Cooper, H., 11, 12, 16, 32
Cooperative Institutional Research Program, 78
Corning, A. D., 12, 13, 14, 53, 60
Couper, M. P., 7, 8, 10, 25, 26, 28, 27, 30, 31, 51, 53
Coverage error, in Web surveys, 25–26
Crask, M. R., 10, 11, 13, 14, 15, 52, 53, 55
Crawford, S. D., 10, 27, 29, 31, 32
Cronbach, L., 86
Cross-sectional studies: advantages and disadvantages of, 79; and age-related differences, 81–82

Data security, and Web-based research, 27–28
de Heer, W., 5, 63
de Leeuw, E., 8

Dey, E., 5, 6, 60
Dillman, D. A., 7, 8, 9, 10, 11, 14, 15, 17, 23, 24, 25, 26, 27, 29, 30, 31, 32, 33, 35, 55, 59, 67, 84, 85
DiLorenzo, T., 79
Dossett, D. L., 16
Duby, P., 53
Durant, L. E., 42, 43
Dyer, J. A., 9

Edwards, B., 65
Electronic surveys: compared with paper surveys, 94–96; cost savings of, 94; development costs of, 93; disadvantages of, 94; equipment costs of, 92; and open-ended questions, 96; and project time, 96. See also E-mail surveys; Web surveys
Ellickson, P. L., 53
E-mail surveys: and data entry performance, 95; options for generating, 91–92; software and shareware for, 92, 93
E-mails, for Web survey follow-up, 31–32
Ethical issues, 27–28, 35
Expedited survey, 45–46
Experimental testing, 6

Fill-in-the-blank (FITB) surveys, 91, 94; handling of open-ended questions in, 95–96
Forthofer, R. N., 16
Fosen, J., 12
Fowler, F. J., 36
Fox, R. J., 10, 11, 13, 15, 16, 52, 53, 55
Frankel, J., 12, 64
Fries, J. C., 27
Fultz, M. L., 6, 13, 65
Furby, L., 86
Furse, D. H., 53, 59

Generation effects, in longitudinal study, 81–82
Gfroerer, 42
Gilmartin, S. K., 26, 27
Glenn, N. D., 76
Golden, L. L., 54
Goldstein, K. M., 11, 12
Gorard, S., 84
Goyder, J. C., 11, 14, 15, 16, 66
Greenberg, D. F., 87
Groves, R. M., 6, 7, 8, 12, 13, 14, 16, 53, 60
Gullickson, A. R., 53

Gunn, H., 23, 28, 32
Gunsalus, C. K., 46
Guterbock, T. M., 27

Handwerk, P., 10, 13
Haraldsen, G., 12
Harris-Kojetin, B., 63
Harrison, L., 42
Hayek, J. C., 9
Hazen, M. D., 9
Heath, F., 13, 31, 53
Heath, R., 23, 32
Heberlein, T. A., 11, 12, 13, 14, 15, 53, 55
Heerwegh, D., 29
Hendel, D. D., 27
Higher Education Research Institute at the University of California-Los Angeles, 76
Hippler, H.-J., 15
Hoogendorn, A. W., 86
Hopkins, K. D., 53
Hox, J., 8
Hoy, M. G., 23
Hubbard, R., 53, 54, 55
Human subject protection, 35; institutional review process for, 46–47, 48; in longitudinal studies, 87; in sensitive-subject surveys, 40
Hyas, R. D., 53

Incentives: and expectation effects, 60; impact of level of, 55–58, 59; in longitudinal studies, 84, 85; lottery, 51, 54–58; monetary, 7, 9; postpaid, 13–14, 53–54, 58–59; prepaid, 13, 52–53; response rate effectiveness of, 51–60; in Web surveys, 32, 51
Informed consent, 87
Institutional environment, and survey participation, 16

James, J. M., 13, 14
James, J., 51, 53, 55, 56
Jennings, M. K., 11, 12
Jobber, D., 53, 56
Johnson, T. E., 24, 27, 32
Jones, S., 34

Kahouse, D. E., 53
Kalton, G., 6, 64
Kanouse, D. E., 13, 84
Kasprzyk, D., 64
Keeling, R. P., 41
Kennedy, J. M., 9

Kessler, R. C., 86
Kim, H., 27, 32
Kim, J., 10, 11, 13, 15, 16, 52, 53, 55
Koch, G., 78
Kojaltic, M., 78
Kropf, M. E., 53, 55
Kuh, G. D., 9, 78
Kwak, N., 27

LaFrance, B., 9
Lagged endogenous variables, 87
Lamias, M. J., 10, 27, 28, 29, 31, 32
LaRose, R., 27
Latham, G. O., 16
Laurie, H., 72, 79, 83
Lea, S., 65
Lepkowski, J. M., 13, 53, 56
Lessler, J., 42
Liang, Q., 79
Little, E. L., 53, 54, 55
Longitudinal panel design, 78–79, 80
Longitudinal studies, 75–88; advantages
    and disadvantages of, 75, 79; appro-
    priateness of, 84; and causal relation-
    ships, 82–83; change scores in,
    86–87; and cohort mortality and
    dropout, 78, 79, 81, 83–84; confiden-
    tiality and informed consent in, 87;
    data handling and analysis in, 86, 88;
    defined, 75; distinction between age,
    period, and time effects in, 81–82;
    funding for, 85, 87–88; and human
    subjects policy, 87; linear panel analy-
    sis in, 82–83; methodology, 75–76;
    planning of, 84–87; response rates in,
    79, 84–85; and sample size, 86; and
    senior campus officials, 85–86;
    sources of error in, 80–82; time con-
    siderations in, 85, 88; types of design
    in, 76–79; and Web surveys, 97
Loosveldt, G., 29
Lorenzi, P., 54
Lott, A., 24, 27, 32, 34

Maher, M. P., 51, 53, 56, 60
Manion, L., 76, 79, 80
Marquis, J. M., 42
Marquis, K. H., 42
Martin, N., 79
Mason, K. O., 86
Mason, W. M., 86
Mathiowetz, N. A., 13, 53, 84
Matier, M., 27, 32
Matross, R. P., 27
McCaffrey, D. F., 53

McCarthy, J. S., 66
McCrory, O. F., 16
McMillen, D. B., 64
Measurement error, 86; in Web surveys,
    26, 28–31, 35
Meekins, B. J., 27
Mehta, R., 9
Menard, S., 76, 78, 79, 82, 83
Miller, E.R.M., 14, 16
Mirza, H., 53
Mitra, A., 9
Mixed–mode survey administration, 35
Mode effects, 26
Monitoring the Future Studies, 78
Moreo, P. J., 9
Mowen, J. C., 15
Multiple contacts, and survey participa-
    tion, 10–11, 59, 67
Multiple surveys, 63–72; and survey
    fatigue, 63, 64; and time concerns, 65

National Center for Education Statistics,
    75
National Commission for the Protection
    of Human Subjects of Biomedical and
    Behavioral Research, 40
National Crime Survey, 78
National Education Longitudinal Studies
    (NELS), 75, 79
National Institute on Alcohol Abuse and
    Alcoholism, 48
National Survey of Youth, 78, 79
Nelson, K., 78
Nesselroade, J. R., 75, 76
Nonresponse bias, in Web surveys,
    25–26, 31
Norm of reciprocity, response rates and,
    8, 13, 56

Optical character recognition (OCR) sur-
    vey, 91; equipment costs for, 92; han-
    dling of open–ended questions in,
    95–96
Optical mark recognition survey (OMR):
    cost and time considerations in,
    94–95; defined, 91; equipment
    requirements for, 92
Ouimet, J. A., 9

Panel studies: data and documentation
    needs in, 86; defined, 75, 76; disad-
    vantages of, 80; multiple cohort design
    in, 78–79; and reciprocal causal influ-
    ences, 82–83; respondent burden in,
    64–65; revolving panel design in, 78

Paolillo, J., 54
Paper surveys: compared with electronic surveys, 94–96; data entry and transmission costs of, 94–95; development costs of, 93; equipment and software costs of, 92; and project time, 96; types of, 91
Parker, R. A., 36
Pascarella, E., 87
Pealer, L. N., 25
Pennell, B., 13, 53, 56
Plewis, I., 86
Polich, J. M., 42
Poole, W. K., 86
Porter, S. R., 16, 32, 54, 87
Presser, S., 36
Privacy, and Web surveys, 27
Project time: in longitudinal studies, 85; in paper versus electronic surveys, 96; and response rates, 64, 65; in Web surveys, 24
Pryor, J., 41

Quality control, in longitudinal studies, 83
Questionnaire, creation of, 44
Questions: open-ended, coding of, 95–96; in sensitive-topic surveys, 30–41

Radler, B. T., 27
Raw change scores, 86
Rea, L. M., 36
Recall errors, 80
Recent College Graduates study, 75
Regression analysis, 86
Repeated cross-sectional design, in longitudinal study, 78
Residual change scores, 86
Resources, on-line, 18
Response rates: decline in, 5–6; demographic characteristics and, 6, 26–27; factors affecting, 8–16; and follow-up reminders, 31–32; in longitudinal studies, 79, 84–85; multiple contacts and, 10–11, 59; prizes' impact on, 13–14, 51–60; and survey fatigue, 64–72; and survey salience, 14, 17; time issues in, 64, 65; in Web-based surveys, 31–33
Respondent burden, and survey fatigue, 64
Retrospective reports, 76
Revolving panel design, in longitudinal study, 78

Roberts, R. E., 16
Rogan, R. G., 9
Roscoe, H. S., 9

Saari, L. M., 16
Salant, P., 36
Sampling error, in Web surveys, 25, 26, 28, 34
Saunders, J., 53, 56
Sax, L. J., 26, 27, 78, 79
Schaefer, D. R., 9, 31, 35, 53, 55
Schaie, K. W., 81
Schlitz, M., 5
Schmidt, W. C., 24, 25
Schroeder, K.E.E., 42, 43
Schuman, H., 13, 53, 56
Schwarz, N., 15
Scott, L., 72, 79, 83
Searcy, S., 24, 27, 32, 34
Sensitive-topic surveys, 39–40; benefits of, 41; choice of instrument in, 43–44; confidentiality and anonymity issues in, 42–43, 47–48; and human subject review, 46–47; methodology, 46–49; privacy concerns in, 40; reporting issues in, 48–49; and response validity, 41–42; risks involved in, 40–41; timing of, 48; types of questions in, 30–41
Sexual behavior research, and response validity, 42
Shahid, A., 79, 80
Shannon, D. M., 9, 24, 27, 32
Sharp, L. M., 12, 64, 65
Sharpe, L. H., 54
Sheehan, K. B., 23
Sikkel, D., 80, 86
Silberstein, A., 5, 65
Sills, S. J., 25
Sinclair, M. D., 11
Singer, E., 12, 13, 14, 51, 53, 54, 56, 60
Singer, J. D., 79
Sivadas, E., 9
Skinner, S. J., 11, 12, 13, 16, 53
Smith, C. B., 27
Smith, K., 11
Smith, R., 72, 79, 83
Smith, T. W., 40, 42
Social desirability effects, and Web surveys, 25
Social exchange theory, 7
Social responsibility norm, survey response rates and, 15
Software, for e–mail and Web surveys, 92–93

Song, C., 25
Sosdian, C. P., 65
"Spamming," 27
Stalnacke, M., 12
Steeh, C. G., 5, 63
Steiger, D. M., 25
Stewart, D. W., 53, 59
Survey administration, multiple contacts in, 10–11, 59, 67
Survey deadlines, response rate and, 16
Survey design, 36; common assumptions about, 17–18; leveraging approach to, 17; paper versus Web, 9–10; Web-based, 24–25, 28; weighted data in, 6, 7
Survey fatigue: and nonpanel survey findings, 65–66; and respondent burden, 64–65; tests of, 66–72
Survey instruments, 63; creation of, 44; for lottery incentives experiment, 55; for sensitive–topic research, 43–44, 45tab; and stakeholder buy-in, 44–46; and use of existing instrument, 43–44
Survey length, response rate and, 11–13, 32
Survey research, demand for, 5
Survey response: and nonresponse bias, 26–27; psychological approach to, 7–8; reasoned action approach to, 7, 8; theories, 6–8. See also Response rates
Survey salience: response rate and, 14, 17; and survey fatigue, 65, 72
Survey sponsorship, 15–16

Technology: and nonresponse bias, 26–27; requirements, in Web–based research, 28
Terenzini, P., 87
Terkla, D. G., 9
Test-retest effects, in longitudinal study, 80, 81
Thompson, R. L., 13, 23, 31, 32, 53
Time issues. See Project time
Time series studies, 75
Tomsic, M. L., 27
Tortora, R. D., 10, 25, 30, 31
Total population design, in longitudinal study, 76–77
Tourangeau, R., 25, 40, 42
Traugott, M. W., 28, 31
Treat, J. B., 14, 15
Trumbo, C. W., 24, 35
Tucker, C., 42, 63

Umbach, P. D., 35, 87
Underwood, D., 27, 32
University of Delaware's Academic Experiences Study, 79, 80, 84–85

van Hoewyk, J., 51, 53, 56, 60
Vesper, N., 78
von Thurn, D. R., 14
Vorst, H., 8

Wall, W. D., 81
Wallace, J., 9
Ward, E. P., 14, 53, 84
Warde, B., 9
Warriner, K., 13, 16, 53, 54, 55, 59
Watt, J. H., 24
Weaver, A. C., 27
Web surveys, 9–10, 23–35; advantages of, 24–25, 96–97; anonymity and, 97; and best practices, 28–31, 33–35; coverage principles and, 28; data entry issues in, 95; design and preparation of, 28, 33–34; disadvantages of, 25–28; e-mail contacts in, 31–32, 33; ethical issues in, 27–28; impact of incentives on, 32; labor costs of, 24; measurement error in, 26, 28–31, 35; response rates of, 97; software for, 93; sources of error in, 25–27, 34; and survey fatigue, 68–72, 97; and technical expertise, 28; time savings of, 24
Web-based resources, 18
Wee, K. H., 53
Weible, R., 9
Weitzer, W. H., 63
Whitcomb, M. E., 16, 32, 63
Whitcomb, M. W., 54
White, A. A., 13, 53, 84
Willet, J. B., 79
Williams, H. C., 81
Willimack, D. W., 12, 53, 56
Winsborough, H. H., 86
Wood, P., 79, 80

Yammarino, F. J., 11, 12, 13, 16, 53
Your First College Year Survey, 78, 79
Yu, J., 11, 12, 16
Yun, G. W., 24, 35

Zanutto, E., 60
Zaslavsky, A., 60
Zhang, Y., 24, 25, 27, 28
Zusman, B. J., 53

Back Issue/Subscription Order Form

Copy or detach and send to:
Jossey-Bass, A Wiley Imprint, 989 Market Street, San Francisco CA 94103-1741

Call or fax toll-free: Phone 888-378-2537 6:30AM – 3PM PST; Fax 888-481-2665

Back Issues: Please send me the following issues at $29 each
(Important: please include ISBN number with your order.)

_____

_____

_____

$ _____ Total for single issues

$ _____

SHIPPING CHARGES: SURFACE	Domestic	Canadian
First Item	$5.00	$6.00
Each Add'l Item	$3.00	$1.50

For next-day and second-day delivery rates, call the number listed above.

Subscriptions Please __ start __ renew my subscription to *New Directions for Institutional Research* for the year 2_____at the following rate:

	Individual	Institutional
U.S.	__ Individual $80	__ Institutional $150
Canada	__ Individual $80	__ Institutional $190
All Others	__ Individual $104	__ Institutional $224
Online Subscription		__ Institutional $150

**For more information about online subscriptions visit
www.interscience.wiley.com**

$ _____ Total single issues and subscriptions (Add appropriate sales tax for your state for single issue orders. No sales tax for U.S. subscriptions. Canadian residents, add GST for subscriptions and single issues.)

__Payment enclosed (U.S. check or money order only)
__VISA __ MC __ AmEx __ # _____ Exp. Date _____

Signature _____ Day Phone _____
__ Bill Me (U.S. institutional orders only. Purchase order required.)

Purchase order # _____
        Federal Tax ID13559302   GST 89102 8052

Name _____

Address _____

_____

Phone _____ E-mail _____

For more information about Jossey-Bass, visit our Web site at **www.josseybass.com**

OTHER TITLES AVAILABLE IN THE
NEW DIRECTIONS FOR INSTITUTIONAL RESEARCH SERIES
J. Fredericks Volkwein, Editor-in-Chief

IR120   **Using Geographic Information Systems in Institutional Research**
Daniel Teodorescu
Exploring the potential of geographic information systems (GIS) applications in
higher education administration, this issue introduces IR professionals and
campus administrators to a powerful presentation and analysis tool. Chapters
explore the benefits of working with the spatial component of data in
recruitment, admissions, facilities, alumni development, and other areas, with
examples of actual GIS applications from several higher education institutions.
ISBN: 0-7879-7281-9

IR119   **Maximizing Revenue in Higher Education**
F. King Alexander, Ronald G. Ehrenberg
This volume presents edited versions of some of the best articles from a forum
on institutional revenue generation sponsored by the Cornell Higher Education
Research Institute. The chapters provide different perspectives on revenue
generation and how institutions are struggling to find an appropriate balance
between meeting public expectations and maximizing private market forces.
The insights provided about options and alternatives will enable campus
leaders, institutional researchers, and policymakers to better understand
evolving patterns in public and private revenue reliance.
ISBN: 0-7879-7221-5

IR118   **Studying Diverse Institutions: Contexts, Challenges, and Considerations**
M. Christopher Brown II, Jason E. Lane
This volume examines the contextual and methodological issues pertaining to
studying diverse institutions (including women's colleges, tribal colleges, and
military academies), and provides effective and useful approaches for higher
education administrators, institutional researchers and planners, policymakers,
and faculty seeking to better understand students in postsecondary education.
It also offers guidelines to asking the right research questions, employing the
appropriate research design and methods, and analyzing the data with respect
to the unique institutional contexts.
ISBN: 0-7879-6990-7

IR117   **Unresolved Issues in Conducting Salary-Equity Studies**
Robert K. Toutkoushian
Chapters discuss the issues surrounding how to use faculty rank, seniority, and
experience as control variables in salary-equity studies. Contributors review the
challenges of conducting a salary-equity study for nonfaculty administrators
and staff—who constitute the majority of employees, even in academic
institutions—and examine the advantages and disadvantages of using
hierarchical linear modeling to measure pay equity. They present a case-study
approach to illustrate the political and practical challenges that researchers
often face when conducting a salary-equity study for an institution. This is a
companion volume to Conducting Salary-Equity Studies: Alternative
Approaches to Research (IR115).
ISBN: 0-7879-6863-3

IR116   **Reporting Higher Education Results: Missing Links in the Performance Chain**
Joseph C. Burke, Henrick P. Minassians
The authors review performance reporting's coverage, content, and customers, they examine in depth the reporting indicators, types, and policy concerns, and they compare them among different states' reports. They highlight weaknesses in our current performance reporting—such as a lack of comparable indicators for assessing the quality of undergraduate education—and make recommendations about how to best use and improve performance information.
ISBN: 0-7879-6336-4

IR115   **Conducting Salary-Equity Studies: Alternative Approaches to Research**
Robert K. Toutkoushian
Synthesizing nearly 30 years of research on salary equity from the field of economics and the experiences of past studies, this issue launches an important dialogue between scholars and institutional researchers on the methodology and application of salary-equity studies in today's higher education institutions. The first of a two-volume set on the subject, it also bridges the gap between academic research and the more pragmatic statistical and political considerations in real-life institutional salary studies.
ISBN: 0-7879-6335-6

IR114   **Evaluating Faculty Performance**
Carol L. Colbeck
This issue brings new insights to faculty work and its assessment in light of reconsideration of faculty work roles, rapid technological change, increasing bureaucratization of the core work of higher education, and public accountability for performance. Exploring successful methods that individuals, institutions, and promotion and tenure committees are using for evaluations of faculty performance for career development, this issue is an indispensable guide to academic administrators and institutional researchers involved in the faculty evaluation process.
ISBN: 0-7879-6334-8

IR113   **Knowledge Management: Building a Competitive Advantage in Higher Education**
Andreea M. Serban, Jing Luan
Provides a comprehensive discussion of knowledge management, covering its theoretical, practical, and technological aspects with an emphasis on their relevance for applications in institutional research. Chapters examine the theoretical basis and impact of data mining; discuss the role of institutional research in customer relationship management; and provide a framework for the integration of institutional research within the larger context of organization learning. With a synopsis of technologies that support knowledge management and an exploration of future developments in this field, this volume assists institutional researchers and analysts in taking advantage of the opportunities of knowledge management and addressing its challenges.
ISBN: 0-7879-6291-0

IR112   **Balancing Qualitative and Quantitative Information for Effective Decision Support**
Richard D. Howard, Kenneth W. Borland Jr.
Establishes methods for integration of numeric data and its contextual application. With theoretical and practical examples, contributors explore the

techniques and realities of creating, communicating, and using balanced decision support information. Chapters discuss the critical role of measurement in building institutional quality; examples of conceptual and theoretical frameworks and their application for the creation of evaluation information; and methods of communicating data and information in relation to its decision support function.
ISBN: 0-7879-5796-8

IR111   **Higher Education as Competitive Enterprise: When Markets Matter**
Robert Zemsky, Susan Shaman, Daniel B. Shapiro
Offers a comprehensive history of the development and implementation of Collegiate Results Instrument (CRI), a tool for mapping the connection between market forces and educational outcomes in higher education. Chapters detail the methods that CRI uses to help institutions to remain value centered by becoming market smart.
ISBN: 0-7879-5795-X

IR110   **Measuring What Matters: Competency-Based Learning Models in Higher Education**
Richard Voorhees
An analysis of the findings of the National Postsecondary Education Cooperative project on data and policy implications of national skill standards, this issue provides researchers, faculty, and academic administrators with the tools needed to deal effectively with the emerging competency-based initiatives.
ISBN: 0-7879-1411-8

IR109   **The Student Ratings Debate: Are They Valid? How Can We Best Use Them?**
Michael Theall, Philip C. Abrami, Lisa A. Mets
Presents a thorough analysis of the use of student evaluations of teaching for summative decisions and discusses the ongoing controversies, emerging research, and dissenting opinions on their utility and validity. Summarizes the role of student ratings as tools for instructional improvement, as evidence for promotion and tenure decisions, as the means for student course selection, as a criterion of program effectiveness, and as the continuing focus of active research and intensive discussion.
ISBN: 0-7879-5756-9

IR108   **Collaboration Between Student Affairs and Institutional Researchers to Improve Institutional Effectiveness**
.J. Worth Pickering, Gary R. Hanson
Defines the unique aspects of student affairs research, including its role in responding to assessment mandates and accreditation agencies, its use of student development theory in formulating research questions, the value of qualitative methods it employs, and the potential contribution it can make to institutional decision making.
ISBN: 0-7879-5727-5

IR107   **Understanding the College Choice of Disadvantaged Students**
Alberto F. Cabrera, Steven M. La Nasa
Examines the college-choice decision of minority and disadvantaged students and suggests avenues to help promote access and improve participation. Explores the influence of family and high school variables as well as racial and ethnic differences on college-choice.
ISBN: 0-7879-5439-X

IR106 Analyzing Costs in Higher Education: What Institutional Researchers
       Need to Know
       Michael F. Middaugh
       Presents both the conceptual and practical information that will give
       researchers solid grounding in selecting the best approach to cost analysis.
       Offers an overview of cost studies covering basic issues and beyond, from a
       review of definitions of expenditure categories and rules of financial reporting
       to a discussion of a recent congressionally mandated study of higher education
       costs.
       ISBN: 0-7879-5437-3

IR105 What Contributes to Job Satisfaction Among Faculty and Staff
       Linda Serra Hagedorn
       Argues that positive outcomes for the entire campus can only be achieved
       within an environment that considers the satisfaction of all of those employed
       in the academy. Examines various jobs within the campus community—
       including classified staff and student affairs administrators as well as faculty—
       and suggests factors that will promote job satisfaction.
       ISBN: 0-7879-5438-1

IR104 What Is Institutional Research All About? A Critical and Comprehensive
       Assessment of the Profession
       J. Fredericks Volkwein
       Chapters explore the role IR plays in improving an institution's ability to learn,
       review organizational behavior theories that shed light on the researcher's
       relationship with the institution, and discuss the three tiers of organizational
       intelligence that make up IR—technical/analytical, contextual, and issues
       intelligence.
       ISBN: 0-7879-1406-1

IR103 How Technology Is Changing Institutional Research
       Liz Sanders
       Illustrates how to streamline office functions through the use of new
       technologies, assesses the impact of distance learning on faculty workload and
       student learning, and responds to the new opportunities and problems posed
       by expanding information access.
       ISBN: 0-7879-5240-0

IR102 Information Technology in Higher Education: Assessing Its Impact and
       Planning for the Future
       Richard N. Katz, Julia A. Rudy
       Provides campus leaders, institutional researchers, and information
       technologists much-needed guidance for determining how IT investments
       should be made, measured, and assessed. Offers practical, effective models for
       integrating IT planning into institutional planning and goals, assessing the
       impact of IT investments on teaching, learning, and administrative operations,
       and promoting efficient information management practices.
       ISBN: 0-7879-1409-6

IR101 A New Era of Alumni Research: Improving Institutional Performance and
       Better Serving Alumni
       Joseph Pettit, Larry L. Litten
       Drawing from information generated by mail and telephone surveys, focus
       groups, and institutional data analysis, the authors examine various facets of an
       institution's relationship with alumni—including fundraising from alumni,
       services for alumni, and occupational and other outcomes of college.
       ISBN: 0-7879-1407-X

Printed in the United States
57996LVS00005B/517

9 780787 974770